PENGUIN

THE RULE OF BENEDICT

BENEDICT, the author of the monastic Rule that bears his name, is known to us only through the account of his life given by Pope Gregory the Great in the second book of his *Dialogues*, written about fifty years after Benedict's death, in which he is portrayed as a great ascetic and miracle worker rather than as the founder of what was to become, over the following centuries, a hugely successful and influential Christian monastic order. From Gregory we learn that Benedict was born in Nursia (now Norcia), some one hundred kilometres north-east of Rome, in about 480 and was sent to Rome for a classical education. However, he became disillusioned with the decadent life-style he encountered in the capital and withdrew to a place of solitude to dedicate his life to God. As his fame spread, he attracted followers whom he organized into small communities of monks before founding the larger monastery at Monte Cassino between Rome and Naples where he spent the rest of his life and where he wrote the Rule for his monks. He died in about 545.

CAROLINNE WHITE was born in London and read Classics and Modern Languages at St Hugh's College, Oxford. She wrote a doctoral thesis on Christian ideas of friendship in the fourth century, published in 1992. After two years spent teaching Latin at the University of South Africa in Pretoria, she returned to Oxford where she worked on the supplement to the Liddell and Scott Greek Lexicon and taught Patristic and Medieval Latin. She now divides her time between work as an assistant editor on the *Dictionary of Medieval Latin from British Sources*, translation work and her four children. Her publications include a translation of the correspondence between Jerome and Augustine (1990), *Early Christian Lives* (Penguin, 1998) and an anthology of *Early Christian Latin Poets* in translation (2000).

The Rule of Benedict

Translated with an Introduction and Notes by
CAROLINNE WHITE

PENGUIN BOOKS

PENGUIN CLASSICS

Published by the Penguin Group
Penguin Books Ltd, 80 Strand, London WC2R ORL, England
Penguin Group (USA) Inc., 375 Hudson Street, New York, New York 10014, USA
Penguin Group (Canada), 90 Eglinton Avenue East, Suite 700, Toronto, Ontario, Canada M4P 2Y3
(a division of Pearson Penguin Canada Inc.)
Penguin Ireland, 25 St Stephen's Green, Dublin 2, Ireland
(a division of Penguin Books Ltd)
Penguin Group (Australia), 250 Camberwell Road, Camberwell, Victoria 3124, Australia
(a division of Pearson Australia Group Pty Ltd)
Penguin Books India Pvt Ltd, 11 Community Centre, Panchsheel Park, New Delhi – 110 017, India
Penguin Group (NZ), 67 Apollo Drive, Rosedale, North Shore 0632, New Zealand
(a division of Pearson New Zealand Ltd)
Penguin Books (South Africa) (Pty) Ltd, 24 Sturdee Avenue, Rosebank, Johannesburg 2196, South Africa

Penguin Books Ltd, Registered Offices: 80 Strand, London WC2R ORL, England

www.penguin.com

This translation published in Penguin Classics 2008

025

Editorial material and translation copyright © Carolinne White, 2008
Set in 10.25/12.25 pt PostScript Adobe Sabon
Typeset by Rowland Phototypesetting Ltd, Bury St Edmunds, Suffolk
Printed and bound in Great Britain by Clays Ltd, Elcograf S.p.A.
ISBN: 978-0-140-44996-9

www.greenpenguin.co.uk

MIX
Paper | Supporting
responsible forestry
FSC® C018179
www.fsc.org

Penguin Books is committed to a sustainable
future for our business, our readers and our planet.
This book is made from Forest Stewardship
Council™ certified paper.

Contents

Contents

THE RULE OF BENEDICT

Introduction

The Rule of Benedict: characteristics and content

The Rule of Benedict, composed in Latin[1] in about 540, provides a practical guide to the Christian monastic life. In it St Benedict transmitted much that he had learned from earlier writers on various aspects of an ascetic life devoted to God as it had developed in the previous two hundred years, as well as from his own experiences, but the outstanding success of his work derived from his ability to combine a clear and inspiring spiritual programme with a concise set of guidelines on practical matters relating to the creation of a harmonious community of individuals, an efficient organization aimed at allowing each individual to make progress in the Christian virtues and to gain eternal life. Although a monastic existence has never been the choice of more than a minority of the population, it gradually grew in importance after Benedict's time, and under the influence of his Rule, it came to play an integral, even dominant part in the European society of the Middle Ages and the formation of its culture. Even today, when the ratio of those living within monastic communities[2] to the rest of the population is far lower than in the Middle Ages, the legacy of that culture is still strong and Benedictine spirituality, drawing on the Rule, continues to help many, even those outside such communities, by giving them insight into their faith and into the human soul, while also offering a structure to the daily Christian life.

In the Prologue Benedict speaks of his intention to create a school for the Lord's service, in which those who have listened to God's call to follow him and to seek his heavenly kingdom will strive to make progress by means of a combination of good works, faith and God's grace, with the Gospels as their guide. It is a school from which a person does not graduate in this life, but by working hard to master Christ's teachings he may win the prize of eternal life. The Prologue is dominated by images of the monastic life as a journey and as a battle in which the monk, armed with faith and good works, is fighting for Christ and striving to progress, with a sense of urgency, along the path to salvation. It may seem strange to choose to spend one's life in such a strict and restricted environment as offered by a monastery, especially since all the biblical guidelines on how to lead a good Christian life (particularly as quoted by Benedict in the Prologue and Chapter 4) would appear to be equally valid outside the monastic context, and yet throughout the Rule he takes for granted not only that what motivates the committed Christian is the desire for eternal life but also that the monastery provides the best conditions in which to work towards fulfilment of this desire.

The routine Benedict proposes for his 'school' revolves round the seven daily services (also known as offices or canonical hours), called Lauds, Prime, Terce, Sext, None, Vespers and Compline,[3] to be performed at set times in the chapel, in addition to the night office.[4] Between these services there will be set times, too, for eating, reading and study (known as *lectio divina*),[5] and periods of manual labour. It is this routine which is often summed up in the proverbial precept associated with the Benedictine life, *ora et labora* ('pray and work'), though it does not appear in this form anywhere in the Rule. Benedict does not deny that such a life is hard, particularly at first, and that problems can arise that threaten to sabotage the enterprise. He admits, for example, that some will find it difficult to get out of bed for the first church service before dawn,[6] some may not feel like reading during the daily quiet period, and some will feel resentment or be stubborn, disobedient or proud. But he believes that under the firm but loving leadership of the abbot, each individual will have the opportunity to learn to practise humility, based on obedience, and to develop his particular talents. Humility is the key to harmony and equality within the community and the virtue to which Benedict devotes one of his longest chapters (7), for by its means a person will reach 'the perfect love of God', allowing him to do everything out of love and a positive desire for virtue rather than from fear. Even the abbot must always behave with humility, listening to advice and being aware of the responsibility he has for the spiritual well-being of each member of his flock.[7] In the words of Basil Hume, 'Humility is a virtue for the strong monk, because it enables him to put God and other people at the centre of his life and not himself.'[8] Although it is the abbot's duty to maintain discipline at all times, he must do so in a spirit of love, pruning away faults without being too harsh: if he rubs too hard to remove the dirt, he may damage the pot, as Benedict warns in Chapter 64. The abbot should give the strong members of the community something to strive for, while not demanding so much from the weaker ones that they become discouraged.

Although Benedict believes that if the abbot is chosen for the goodness of his life and the wisdom of his teaching, and if he does everything in accordance with Christ's teachings,[9] all should be well in the community, he does admit that things can go wrong in the relations between abbot and community. It may happen that the community will elect as its abbot someone who turns a blind eye to their faults, in which case the local bishop must intervene. On the other hand it may happen that the abbot, despite his best efforts, is unable to correct the faults he finds in the members of his community, in which case he has to accept that it must be left to God to punish them on the Day of Judgement. Benedict himself had experienced such a situation when he was asked by a community to replace their abbot who had recently died. Reluctantly he agreed to do so but both parties soon became disillusioned: Benedict imposed a strict way of life but found the monks most unwilling to accept this. They became furious that 'under his leadership unlawful things were no longer lawful'[10] and so they plotted to murder him. However, when they poisoned his wine, Benedict was saved by the miraculous shattering of the wine glass before he could take a sip.

This chilling incident is recounted by Pope Gregory the Great, who wrote an account of the miracles associated with Benedict some fifty years after his death. This narrative, drawn from the personal memories of four of Benedict's disciples and contained in Book 2 of Gregory's *Dialogues*, provides our only details of Benedict's life. We hear of his tender relationship with his nurse and his sister, but nothing about his parents except that they were free-born and could clearly afford to send their son to Rome for his education. Gregory makes much of Benedict's rejection, as a young man, of his family's ambitions for him in favour of solitude and dedication to God.[11] Solitude was to remain his ideal, but he attracted to himself many followers for whom he is said to have organized twelve monasteries, each containing twelve monks[12] under the supervision of an abbot. And yet, despite the fact that solitude was Benedict's starting point, he makes it clear in Chapter 1 of the Rule that he believes that Christians need to be trained first within the solidarity of the communal monastic life. He himself spent much of his life as abbot in the large monastery he had founded, high up on Monte Cassino,[13] between Rome and Naples, where he wrote the Rule and where he died in about 545.

In Gregory's *Dialogues* Benedict comes across as austere but kindly, as we see him using his gifts of healing and prophecy in a calm and unsensational manner, whether in dealing with the celebrities and powerful people of his age who came to visit him, or with the local country people, in this period of political turbulence after the break-up of the Roman Empire when emperor Justinian was struggling to wrest Italy from the control of the Goths. Gregory praises him not only for the miracles which made him famous throughout the world but also for the wisdom of his teaching and for the Rule 'which is remarkable for its discretion and the clarity of its language'.[14] In the background we catch glimpses of Benedict and his disciples living according to his Rule: praying, both communally and in solitude; keeping to the times of the daily services of psalm-singing and prayer; reading; building the chapels, guest-houses and refectories necessary for the monasteries, clearing weeds from the garden, fetching water, working in the fields; visiting other monasteries to offer spiritual encouragement, while taking care not to eat any meals on the way, as the Rule stipulates in

Chapter 51; and offering hospitality to others. We also see him at a moment when perhaps his allegiance to duty and rules caused him to fail in the principal ideal of love, in which his sister Scholastica showed herself to be the stronger. She had been consecrated to God as a child[15] and visited her brother once a year. As women were not allowed in the monastery, brother and sister would meet at a house outside the monastery and spend the day in prayer and holy conversation. Benedict always returned to his monastery in the evening, but on one occasion Scholastica begged him to stay with her and continue their conversation through the night. Benedict felt this was against the rules and refused her request, so Scholastica, in tears, prayed that the clear weather would change and make his departure impossible. The moment her prayer finished, the rain started to pour down and the thunderstorm forced Benedict to stay and spend the whole night discussing spiritual matters. Gregory comments that 'contrary to his wishes, the power of the almighty God caused him to discover a miracle produced by a woman's heart. It is not surprising that a woman was able to achieve more than him at that time, seeing that she had long desired to see her brother. For according to the words of John, *God is love*, and so it was by a very just judgement that her power was greater because her love was stronger.'[16]

How central a place did love hold in Benedict's vision? Certainly, he takes the twofold commandment to love God and neighbour, the importance of which was stressed by Christ,[17] and places it at the start of Chapter 4, in which he gives a long list of the things the monks ought to do or avoid doing in this life in order to express their love of God and to win the reward of eternal life, and yet the Prologue makes obedience the key that will allow one to reach God. In Chapter 7 Benedict places love for God as the third rung on the ladder to humility, recognizing that love must be the motive as well as the goal, and yet there it is placed in the context of an exhortation to obedience. In Chapter 72 he warmly encourages the monks to love each other with mutual respect and patience, and yet this follows immediately after a chapter in which Benedict wrote that 'the virtue of obedience is not only to be practised by all towards the abbot but the brothers must also obey each other, aware that it is by walking along the path of obedience that they will reach God.' Nowhere does Benedict explicitly base his view of monastic life in the community on the duty to love one's neighbour, as St Basil and St Augustine had:[18] for Benedict it is as if the monastery happens to be a community merely as a result of being a kind of boarding school. But for him obedience and love are not contradictory but inextricably linked.

This is evident also in the chapters of the Rule dealing with discipline and punishment.[19] Benedict provides a series of measures to eradicate error and sin as soon as they spring up, starting with an attempt to correct by means of a reprimand from the abbot in private and moving on through public rebuke in front of all the brothers, exclusion from the common meal, exclusion from the sacraments and church services, and finally corporal punishment, if it is felt that previous attempts at correction were unsuccessful and the punishments too lenient. In Chapter 71 Benedict indicates that if a monk is so stubborn that even corporal punishment fails to bring him into line,[20] then he will have to be expelled from the monastery. No doubt it was hoped that adult monks could mostly be corrected by means of a discreet rebuke.

As for the boys,[21] handed over to the monastery by their parents for training in the monastic life, they were more likely to be punished by being beaten or deprived of meals. In addition to such physical measures, there were also emotional hardships to be endured by the boys: they were not allowed to receive any letters or presents from their parents without the abbot's permission, and even if the abbot allowed a present, he had the right to decide to give it to someone else! No one was allowed to defend anyone else or say a kind word to one who was being punished, even if it was a close relative. If such treatment seems harsh and open to abuse by those in charge, it should be remembered that Benedict does at least state that no one is allowed to treat the boys too harshly. In other ways, too, he makes special provision for the boys, taking account of their weaknesses while maintaining discipline: they are to sleep in separate beds, with older monks close at hand to supervise them, and a candle is to be kept burning through the night; if they are hungry they are allowed to eat before the others, though they will be given smaller portions than the adults.

As with the relation between love and obedience, so with the relation between the Gospels and the rest of the Bible. Although the Rule is often described as an epitome of Gospel teaching and it is true that Chapter 4 in particular contains many moral precepts that reflect Christ's teachings, it would be misleading to emphasize the Gospels at the expense of the rest of the Bible. The variety of Benedict's citations is remarkable, as is the virtuosity with which he works the citations into the text. The divine office, to which the monks devote so much of their time, is based primarily on the singing of the psalms (in Chapter 18 Benedict advises that all 150 psalms should be recited each week, though he admits that this represents a fall in standards as in the past many recited all the psalms every day), together with readings and prayers from other parts of the Bible. The Scriptural texts quoted by Benedict throughout the Rule to give authority to his advice and exhortations are taken not only from Christ's teachings in the Gospels, but also from the Old Testament and from St Paul's letters. In fact, only about one-fifteenth of the citations derive from the Gospels. Benedict uses the Scriptural citations in various ways. Many of them are in the form of direct advice, with God, Christ or St Paul as it were addressing the individual and telling him how to behave; others are in the form of proverbial statements, often drawn from the Wisdom literature of the Old Testament, including the Apocrypha, offering some truth about human life or the relation between man and God; and still others, usually taken from the psalms, are more personal, allowing each individual monk to express his thoughts and feelings to God in the words of the psalmist, who frequently addressed God directly with sentiments common to the human condition. On occasion, Benedict will quote a series of short passages from various parts of the Bible to reinforce what he is saying on a particular subject: we thereby see how familiar he was with the whole Bible, in that he can pick out those phrases and sentences relevant to the theme in question. For example in Chapter 7 on the subject of humility, he warns the monks that God can see into their hearts and knows all their thoughts: he proceeds to quote phrases from five psalms expressing this in different ways, in order to inspire them with fear of God. Later in the same chapter Benedict encourages the monks to persevere through the difficulties of monastic life, giving eight quotations (from the Psalms and St Paul's letters, together with one from the Gospel of St Matthew) to illustrate the truth that hardships are to be expected but that God will also provide support.

By the end of the Rule we are left with a positive and humane vision, in which mutual respect and love among the monks, sharing of all property, care for the weak and hospitality shown to strangers emerge as fundamental to the monastic way of life, alongside worship of God. Benedict's Rule, demanding and disciplined as it is, perhaps reveals its author as more flexible and compassionate in his treatment of the monks than he was in dealing with his sister.

Monasticism before Benedict

If Benedict was torn between his desire for solitude and his perception of the value of community life, as the early chapters of Gregory's account imply, he was experiencing a tension found in monasticism from an early stage of its development. At a time when Christianity was becoming increasingly popular as it became first an accepted and then the official religion of the Roman Empire during the course of the fourth century, more and more people felt attracted to a way of life that really tested the devotion of the Christian, in a way that martyrdom had done during the earlier periods of persecution. It seems that the first impulse towards a life of devotion to God led men like Antony and Paul of Egypt, in the third century, to leave the comforts and responsibilities of family life in search of solitude in the vast Egyptian desert, where they could devote themselves fully to God without distraction. They might be motivated by the threat of persecution from pagan authorities, as in the case of Paul, or by a sense of vocation, as in the case of Antony, who took to heart the words of the Gospel, 'If you wish to be perfect, go, sell your possessions and give the money to the poor, and you will have treasure in heaven; then come, follow me', when he heard them read in church.[22] The irony was that before long, news spread throughout the Roman Empire of the fact that these men, by choosing to lead lives of harsh asceticism in remote places, were turning love of God into an extreme sport. As a result their detachment from the world became compromised by those who sought them out: many people decided to visit hermits out of curiosity or in order to learn from them. This meant that on the one hand Antony found his solitude disturbed and felt it necessary to move further and further into the desert to preserve his way of life; and on the other there began a colonization of the desert[23] by individuals and small groups of would-be monks, which was followed, at the end of the fourth century, by flourishing tourism throughout the deserts of Egypt and Syria, and visits to the monks which could be combined with pilgrimages to the Holy Land. It was as if the plants of a new religion were growing in the sterile soil of the desert, as one sixteenth-century writer[24] described the rapid development of monasticism in its earliest phase.

The idea of a more organized community life, developing out of the loose groups of solitary monks living in the desert, is usually associated with Pachomius, an Egyptian converted to Christianity while a conscript in the Roman army in the early fourth century. He too spent some time imitating Antony's way of life: Palladius in his *Lausiac History* writes that as Pachomius was sitting alone in his cave an angel appeared to him and said, 'Now that you have successfully ordered your own life, you do not need to sit here any longer. Get up, and go and collect together all the young monks and live together with them.'[25] The set of buildings he constructed on cultivated land by the Nile at Tabennisis (probably near the modern town of Qena, north of Luxor) seems to have been the first example of what would become the stereotypical monastery, with a chapel for communal worship, a refectory for communal meals, a guest-house, sick-room, kitchens and houses, in each of which about forty monks could sleep in separate cells or dormitories. It is said that even Antony, the chief proponent of the solitary life, gave the Pachomian monastery his seal of approval, and indeed it proved so popular that by the mid-fourth century daughter monasteries were springing up all along the Nile. Pachomius not only invented a new type of environment in which to devote oneself to God; he also provided a set of rules for this way of life. This seems to have been originally written in Coptic, then translated into Greek, from which St Jerome translated it into Latin at the beginning of the fifth century. In this form it assisted those Latin-speaking people who were joining the monasteries at the time and then spread through western Europe in the following centuries. The 144 sections in Jerome's version[26] deal with all kinds of details of the organized monastic life. Anyone seeking to join is expected to stand outside the monastery patiently for several days, learning the Lord's Prayer and as many psalms as he can before he is allowed to enter. Then, after a period of vetting and instruction, the monk would live in one of the houses under the care of a supervisor to whom he must be obedient, content with the few clothes and utensils given to him by the abbot. He would spend much of his time in agricultural work, in making ropes, mats or baskets, or in the preparation of food, praying silently as he worked. All of this was regarded as the service of God. However, no one was expected to do more than he could sensibly manage. Twice a day all the monks from the different houses would meet for communal prayer and psalm-singing, but Pachomius' liturgical instructions are far less comprehensive and precise than those found in Benedict's Rule. It is interesting that Pachomius makes it clear that all monks have to learn to read if they cannot already do so on entry to the monastery. He not only gives instructions as to what the monks should do, but also as to what is not permitted. They must not talk or laugh at times of prayer, reading or at mealtimes. They must not eat any food before it has been properly distributed to everyone: if, for example, they come across windfall apples, they must not taste them but pile them beside the tree and then give them to the monk responsible for distribution. If a monk travels outside the monastery on some errand, on his return he must not tell anyone what he has experienced. Monks should not wash their whole body unless they are ill, and they must not wash anyone else unless told to do so. They must not share a sleeping mat with anyone else or hold hands. Already the monastic virtues of obedience, chastity and poverty are emerging,[27] although the monks were not expected to take vows.

In the life of Antony (251–356), as depicted by Athanasius of Alexandria shortly after Antony's death, we have the model of the extreme eremitic, or solitary, life. In the monastic organization of Pachomius, who died in 346, we have the blueprint for the coenobitic, or community, life. The intense development of the monastic way of life through the next two centuries, as it spread out of Egypt and the Holy Land to the Near East, Italy, North Africa and Gaul, produced different manifestations of these models. Despite the variations, one can see that each was an attempt, often influenced by the author's or founder's own personality and experiences, to combine what were implicitly regarded as the crucial virtues to be sought in the monastic way of life. The fundamental question concerned the relative value of the eremitic and coenobitic versions: most concluded that the solitary life should only be embarked on after long training in a community. Within the coenobitic life certain virtues and practices become central, though different writers place slightly different emphases on them. These are the virtues of obedience and humility, mutual love, the renunciation of one's own will and one's property, and silence, with less explicit concentration on poverty and chastity than was later to become the norm. Some writers emphasize a hierarchical structure within the monastery, highlighting obedience and the importance of the abbot; others stress the importance of mutual love between all members of the community. Most consider manual labour to be a necessary and spiritually valuable part of the monastic routine, alongside study and the performance of prayer, though they vary in the amount of time allocated to these activities.

One of the earliest works on the monastic life to be written after the period of Antony and Pachomius and which took an unequivocally positive view of community life, was the double set of rules composed in Greek by Basil of Caesarea (330–79) and translated into Latin by Rufinus in about 400. Basil had visited Egypt, Palestine and Syria after leaving university, to learn at first hand about the ascetic life for which these areas were famous. Returning home to what is now Turkey, he started to live an ascetic life in a community of family members and friends, and from his experiences developed his monastic vision. According to W. K. L. Clarke, the editor of his ascetic writings, Basil 'brought the spirit of Antony and the forms devised by Pachomius fused into an harmonious whole ... adding a professional knowledge of the letter and spirit of Scripture'.[28] At the beginning of the longer set of rules, composed in the 360s or 370s and comprising 55 paragraphs dealing mainly with behaviour and personal relations,[29] Basil provides a clear rationale for the monastic life based on the two primary commandments of the Christian life: love of God, he argues, demands separation from the sinful world, while love of neighbour demands that life be shared with other like-minded people. The main characteristics of the way of life Basil recommends are humility, obedience, and a striving for restraint with regard to such things as food, money, sex and anger. Basil also provides practical advice with regard to suitable clothing and food and the punishment of bad behaviour, together with guidelines for communal prayer which should take place seven times during the day in addition to one service at night. This is one of the works that had a powerful influence on Benedict's Rule and indeed Benedict, in his final chapter, recommends the reading of it as teaching us a 'direct route to our creator'.

By the end of the fourth century, interest in the monastic life was spreading to the West and the Latin-speaking area of the Roman Empire. The first monastic rule we have that was written originally in Latin is the Rule of St Augustine, comprising the brief *Ordo Monasterii* (or *Regula Secunda*) and the eight chapters of the *Praeceptum*, which, like the Rule of Benedict, give a biblical foundation for the monastic life as well as rules regarding the daily timetable of prayer and work, discipline and correct behaviour towards others. Augustine had been powerfully influenced by his reading of Athanasius' *Life of Antony* in his painful decision to embark on a Christian life that rejected marriage and a worldly career, and yet he did not choose to adopt a solitary life but one inspired by his belief in the importance of Christian friendship. Like Basil, Augustine sets the double commandment of love of God and of neighbour at the head of his Rule, adding the injunction to emulate the early Christians at Jerusalem who held all things in common and who were of one heart and one mind, according to the Acts of the Apostles (4:32). Love, unity and equality are central to the Augustinian community. He warns those brothers who had been wealthy in their secular lives against feelings of pride and superiority, and those who came from poorer backgrounds he exhorts not to feel proud that they are associating with people of higher social status.[30] However, such equality within the community does not mean that individual differences are disregarded: each must be treated according to his personal needs. Augustine urges those who are healthy not to envy the sick for the special treatment accorded to them, while those who are sick are not to feel conceited. In this connection he gives a piece of advice which could apply to the whole monastic tradition: it is better to need less than to have more.[31] Despite the enormous influence of Augustine's writings generally and the fact that his Rule clearly survived and was copied in manuscripts, it seems that it was not until the end of the eleventh century that it began to be widely adopted in various communities as an alternative to the Benedictine Rule, at a time when new forms of monastic life were being investigated in the wake of ecclesiastical and monastic reforms. In the following centuries it was to be adopted not only by the Augustinian (or 'Austin') canons, but also by the Premonstratensians and in a modified form by the Dominican friars.[32]

At the same time as Augustine's writings were inspiring the formation of monastic communities in North Africa in the late fourth and early fifth centuries, similar developments were occurring in Gaul under the influence of men such as Martin at Tours, Honorius on the island of Lérins off modern-day Cannes, and Cassian at Marseille. Martin (d. 397) adopted the semi-eremitic life and continued to live a monastic life even after he was made bishop, surrounded by monks in individual cells who came together for a common meal and prayer and who lived simply on what was donated by the local church, so that the necessity of performing manual labour would not distract them from prayer and missionary work.[33] John Cassian (c. 365–435), however, considered that such a system was detrimental to the development of the monastic life.

It was in fact Cassian's picture of the ideal monastic life, as set out in his two major works, the *Institutes* and the *Conferences*, that was to have perhaps the greatest influence on Benedict and the monks who followed his rule. It is from the *Conferences*, written about a century before Benedict's Rule, that Benedict advises that a few pages should be read aloud to the monks after supper[34] and before Compline each day, while in his final chapter he modestly presents his own rule as only possibly of use to those wishing to make a start along the road to perfection, while those who wish to fast-track along this road he advises to study not only Scripture and the theology of the Church Fathers, but also the *Conferences* and *Institutes* of Cassian and the *Rules* of Basil. The *Institutes* is a work in twelve books, the first four of which provide practical information regarding the daily life of a monk – what he is to wear, what prayers and psalms he is to say and when, and how a would-be monk is to be accepted into the community. The next eight books deal with the eight principal vices[35] that threaten the way of life of monks, both in solitude and in community. In many ways, it is the practical advice of the first four books of the *Institutes* that provides most of the material for the Rule of Benedict: in later centuries these were abbreviated and appeared as a separate work, entitled 'The Rule of Cassian'. In both Benedict's Rule and the opening books of the *Institutes*, the emphasis placed on perfect humility and obedience may appear to obscure the fact that these virtues are in fact the means to an end. It is in the twenty-four books of the *Conferences*, a work of great psychological perceptiveness, that Cassian offers a more profound view – as it were a theology of the monastic life. He transmits a synthesis of Egyptian teachings on the monastic life along with those of St Basil, focusing on such topics as the ability to distinguish between good and bad, vices, prayer, friendship, and the different benefits of the solitary life and life in community. The aim of the monk, as is made very clear in Book 1, is to attain purity of heart and perfect love that will allow him to reach the kingdom of heaven and eternal life: all the elements of the monastic life – prayer, meditation on Scripture, silence, manual labour, restriction of the amount of food and sleep – are the practical means of bringing about that purity of heart which may enable the monk, already in this life, to have a foretaste of the blessedness of the next.

There is one document containing guidelines for the monastic life that bears an even more striking resemblance to Benedict's Rule, with similar quotations from the Bible and a similar emphasis on the virtues of obedience, silence and humility. It is also the first work we know that mentions the twelve steps of humility which Benedict lays out in Chapter 7.[36] And yet Benedict makes no mention of it. It was long thought that it may have been a later reworking of his Rule, but the consensus now seems to be that it was written by an unknown writer a few years earlier than his, in other words around the beginning of the sixth century, in the vicinity of Rome, which would make it plausible for Benedict to be familiar with it when he was writing. It is known as *The Rule of the Master*,[37] as it takes the form, popular in this period, of a prolonged question-and-answer session between pupil and master. About three times the length of Benedict's Rule, it is much more expansive in its teachings and also covers additional topics, such as a commentary on the Lord's Prayer, advice on how to wake the abbot for the service by tapping his feet and on wet dreams. In Chapter 5 it also gives a list of thirty-three vices not included by Benedict in the list of rules for virtuous behaviour that comprise his fourth chapter. In general Benedict tends to reproduce what the Master says on spiritual matters, though usually in a drastically abbreviated form, as in the first seven chapters, while on practical and liturgical matters he is more likely to adopt an original position.

The Rule after Benedict's time

And so Benedict, familiar with many of these texts and blending elements drawn from them, composed his Rule for the monks in his monasteries, which over the next few centuries would spread throughout Europe, with the effect that an important new stratum of educated people was introduced into society. But what happened to Benedict's Rule after his death? The *Chronicle of Monte Cassino* states that in the year Benedict died (about 545) he was asked to send some of his monks to Gaul to build a monastery; he agreed to send brother Maurus[38] and as a result Benedict's Rule was disseminated throughout Gaul. However, there is no independent evidence for this, and it is likely that it was only Benedict's own monasteries in southern Italy that lived according to the Rule – until 581 when the monks at Monte Cassino, roused from sleep, were forced to flee to Rome as Lombard invaders arrived to burn down the monastery.[39] It may be that from Rome Benedict's Rule was transported to England during Gregory's time as pope, if the man he sent to England to convert the Anglo-Saxons in 597, known to posterity as Augustine of Canterbury, took a copy with him to use in the monastery he founded at Canterbury. However that may be, it is certain that the Rule was adopted in England some decades later, in the mid-seventh century, and introduced into pre-existing and new monasteries by Wilfrid, abbot of Ripon and bishop of York, and Benedict Biscop, founder of the monasteries of Wearmouth and Jarrow.[40] Although the influence of earlier Irish monasticism, with its emphasis on austerity and mission work, as developed by such men as Columban, who spread it in France, Switzerland and northern Italy, and who was himself the author of two monastic rules, and Columba, who founded Iona off the west coast of Scotland not long after Benedict founded Monte Cassino, continued to be felt in England, after the Synod of Whitby in 664 most English monasteries turned towards Rome and chose to follow the Benedictine Rule. This is the period, too, when women began to live in communities organized according to a mixed set of rules, which incorporated aspects of the Rule: an early example is Hilda, abbess of Whitby, who was in charge of a double monastery of men and women. In the eighth century the Englishman Boniface took Christianity and Benedictine monasticism to northern Europe. But although life in these monasteries was loosely based on Benedict's Rule, observance of it did not become uniform until the early ninth century when a Visigothic nobleman, who had adopted the name Benedict when he founded a monastery on his estate at Aniane in southern France, was asked by Charlemagne's son Louis the Pious to spread knowledge of the Rule throughout the monasteries of the Holy Roman Empire. Benedict of Aniane set out a programme of reforms differing from the original Rule only with regard to details, such as an increased emphasis on contemplation and the performance of the divine office, with the addition of fifteen psalms before the night office and perhaps also the daily recitation of the office of the dead.

But while Benedictine monasticism was beginning to take off on the Continent, monasteries in England were weakened by the repeated Viking invasions that caused so much destruction and social upheaval during the ninth and tenth centuries. It was not until the reforms of Dunstan and Aethelwold in the late tenth century that English monasteries were given a firm organizational and economic foundation, inspired by the vitality of Continental monasteries such as Cluny and Fleury. However, the latter became victims of their own success: as they grew in size and wealth, they too reached a point where they needed to be brought back to the simple rules laid down by Benedict. Reform movements led, for example, to the foundation of the Cistercians in 1098, who aimed to live according to Benedict's Rule more strictly than their contemporaries and did so in more remote areas. Despite such reforms monasteries continued to be vulnerable to external forces, such as wars and secular intervention (as with the dissolution of the monasteries in the sixteenth century in England and in the wake of the French Revolution on the Continent), as well as to internal weakening and corruption as their wealth increased. The delicate balance instituted by Benedict between the time devoted to the divine office and periods of study, manual labour and refreshment, both providing healthy variety in the daily routine, was lost as servants or lay brothers took over the domestic chores, and schools and universities replaced the monasteries as places of learning. The repeated reform programmes, together with the accounts left by bishops whose duty it was to visit monasteries to report any irregularities, and the satirical literature of the Middle Ages, provide us with insights into the ways in which Benedict's Rule suffered distortions. For example in 1238 Pope Gregory IX announced certain reform measures to the assembled abbots of England: these included rules to the effect that no one under the age of twenty should take monastic vows, no one should be charged an entry fee to become a monk, once a year there should be a public excommunication of any monk who held property, and nuns who punched other nuns or clerics required absolution from their local bishop, as well as reminders that Benedict's rules regarding attendance at services and mealtimes, periods of silence and communal sleeping arrangements were to be respected.[41] Monasteries were often saddled with abbots who failed miserably in setting a good example: Benedict would not have been too impressed by abbot Clarembald who became a cause célèbre in the twelfth century for allegedly spending on himself the money received for accepting monastic recruits and the large sums collected for repairs to the church and monastery, as well as fathering seventeen illegitimate children in one village.[42] Monks were often warned not to frequent taverns or gamble (or were derided in the satirical literature for doing so) and nuns not to dress in the latest fashions. Convents such as the one at Godstow outside Oxford became infamous (though no doubt much appreciated by some) for the excessive hospitality lavished on male visitors.[43] Another irregularity that Benedict had not countenanced was the keeping of pets, particularly common in convents: after visiting Romsey Abbey in 1387, Bishop William of Wykeham complained that he had found that 'some of the nuns ... bring with them to church birds, rabbits, dogs ... and pay more attention to them than to the Divine Office, with the result that they find it difficult to sing the psalms'.[44] Langland gives us a picture of squabbling nuns, and Chaucer, in the Prologue to

The Canterbury Tales, depicts a monk who does not care a fig for Benedict's Rule.[45]

It would seem that the dissolution of the monasteries over the subsequent centuries served to purge the monastic life, sweeping away many of the conditions that had led to abuse of the Rule. When Benedictine monasticism was revived in Europe in the early nineteenth century, for the sake of the education provided by the monasteries or as a result of the religious revival in the post-Enlightenment era, it was in a sparer, more focused form. Monasteries had a clear constitution and were grouped in 'congregations' within which they provided mutual support, while being allowed a good deal of autonomy and flexibility in the practice of the Rule. The danger with this is that it allows a monastery to deal with its own problems and this may be done in a less than satisfactory way, but at least there was also a stronger awareness that the monastic life would not suit everybody: the relatively few men and women who chose to adopt it were more likely to do so out of a true sense of vocation.[46]

Until now those who have read Benedict's Rule and written on it, have largely been those closely associated with Benedictine monasticism, but it is time for the Rule to become more widely known beyond this community, to be more accessible to lay people and those of other faiths. The Rule is of interest not only as a source of spiritual inspiration for our daily lives, powerfully persuasive of the importance of silence in our busy routines, and humility and respect in our relations with others,[47] but also as a key text in the history of monasticism and the Christian church.

NOTES

For full bibliographical details, see Further Reading. *RB* is the text of *The Rule of Benedict* in this volume.

1. Benedict's Latin, in its spelling and syntax, seems to reflect accurately his status as an educated sixth-century Christian for whom

Latin was his mother tongue. His style is strongly influenced by the Bible and some of the writings of early Christian authors, such as Augustine in his sermons and Jerome in his lives of the early desert fathers. It is less artificial and complex than that of, for example, Boethius and Cassiodorus, who were roughly his contemporaries. The spelling, as recorded in some of the manuscripts (e.g. those of the 'authentic' text – see Note on the Text), seems unfamiliar to those brought up on what is now regarded as classical Latin, i.e. the Latin of about five hundred years before Benedict's time.

2. Statistics published in 2000 by the Benedictine Order indicate that there are about 8,000 Benedictine monks worldwide and about 14,000 nuns. These numbers do not include lay associates of the Order.

3. Lauds, which derives its name from the Latin word for 'praise' (see Chapter 12, note 2) took place just before daybreak; Prime, Terce, Sext and None were so called because they originally took place at the first, third, sixth and ninth hours of the day; Vespers was held in the early evening; the final service was Compline, for which the Latin term was 'Completorium', derived from the word 'to complete, finish'.

4. Chapters 8–20 of *RB* provide detailed information on the times and content of services, together with advice on the correct behaviour of the monk in church. The collective term used by Benedict for these services is *opus Dei* (work of God). Nowadays the usual term is 'divine office'. The word 'office', meaning a form of worship, derives from the Latin *officium*, meaning a duty, task or service. The routine of seven daily services, which developed gradually in the early Christian church, particularly in the monastic context, is explained in Chapter 16 as having been inspired by the text of Ps. 119:164, 'Seven times a day have I praised you', while the additional night office is given biblical justification by Ps. 119: 62, 'In the middle of the night I rose to praise you.'

5. In *RB* the term *lectio divina* is used (Chapter 48 and note). About two hours a day is to be devoted to this practice of studying and meditating on Scripture, with more time allocated during Lent. Benedict says nothing specifically about how the books to be used would be procured and gives no instructions about the copying of manuscripts (though in Chapter 33 he does speak of the monks not being allowed books, writing tablets or pens of their own but being dependent on the abbot for any supplies they

might need), but it is clear that each monastery must have had a store of books sufficient to allow the monks to have one book each. The distribution of books at the beginning of Lent is described in some detail by Lanfranc in his Monastic Constitutions (*The Monastic Constitutions of Lanfranc*, ed. and trans. D. Knowles, rev. edn. C. N. L. Brooke (London: Thomas Nelson, 1951; reprinted Oxford: Clarendon Press, 2002), pp. 29–31), written in the eleventh century for the Benedictine monks in Canterbury:

> On the first Sunday of Lent ... the librarian should have all the books except those that were given out for reading the previous year collected on a carpet in the chapter-house; last year's books should be carried in by those who have had them. The passage from the Rule of St Benedict concerning the observance of Lent shall be read and ... the librarian shall read out a list of the books which the brothers had the previous year. When each hears his name read out he shall return the book which was given to him and anyone who is conscious that he has not read in full the book he received shall confess his fault prostrate and ask for pardon. Then the librarian shall give to each of the brothers another book to read.

The copying of manuscripts was soon to become an important part of the monastic routine – in fact, it became a form of the manual labour to which at least some of the monks were assigned. (See, e.g., C. H. Lawrence, *Medieval Monasticism* (London and New York: Longman, 1984), pp. 115–18).

6. The twelfth-century writer Nigel Longchamp makes Burnellus the ass, the protagonist of his satirical poem *A Mirror for Fools*, speculate on which monastic order he might join. When he considers the Benedictines, one point he mentions is the need to get up for the night office:

> If I should take a robe that's black
> and live and die a Cluniac ...
> At midnight they will wake me up,
> and turn me out of bed when I
> would go on sleeping cosily.
> (trans. J. H. Mozley (Oxford: B. H. Blackwell,
> 1961), lines 2076–80)

7. Peter the Venerable, abbot of the Benedictine monastery of Cluny, writing in 1137 to his friend the prior of the Carthusians, expresses his fears at the awesome responsibility, aware that he will have to give an account on the Day of Judgement not only of his own moral and spiritual state but also of all the thousands of monks in his charge (Peter the Venerable, *Selected Letters*, ed. Janet Martin (Toronto: Pontifical Institute of Medieval Studies, 1974), Letter 24).

8. Basil Hume, *In Praise of Benedict* (London: Hodder and Stoughton, 1981), p.21.

9. *RB*, Chapters 2 and 64 are particularly concerned with the duties of the abbot. See also Timothy Fry in Appendix 2 of *RB 1980*.

10. Gregory the Great, *Life of Benedict* (= *Dialogues*, Book 2), 3.3 (*Early Christian Lives* (hereafter *ECL*), p. 170).

11. Ibid., Prologue (*ECL* p. 165).

12. Ibid., 3.13 (*ECL* p. 172).

13. Gregory the Great mentions the foundation of Monte Cassino on the hilltop (8.10, *ECL* p. 178). The impregnability of the site is well illustrated by the story, recorded by Matthew Paris in the thirteenth century (*Chronica Majora*, ed. H. R. Luard, Rolls Series (London: Longman and Co., 1876), 3.538), of the thirteen monks who appeared before Pope Gregory IX in 1239 to complain that they had been expelled from Monte Cassino by the emperor, although they were used to controlling access to the monastery. It turned out that the emperor had only managed to enter by using a sort of Trojan Horse trick: he made one of his men feign death so that he could be carried up to Monte Cassino in a coffin. The man then jumped out and overpowered the thirteen unsuspecting monks.

   However, the monastery did not escape becoming the target of Allied bombing in 1944, which reduced it to rubble. It was rebuilt and at the monastery's consecration in 1964, Pope Paul VI proclaimed Benedict the patron saint of Europe.

14. Gregory the Great, *Life of Benedict*, 36 (*ECL* p. 202).

15. It is likely that Scholastica lived at first as a dedicated virgin in their family home, as was usual in early female monasticism. At the time of this episode she is living in a 'cella' (cell), a word that, like monastery, could be applied to a small building, a single room or a monastery.

16. Gregory the Great, *Life of Benedict*, 33 (*ECL* pp. 198–200).

17. New Testament references to the centrality of love of God and neighbour are found in the opening paragraph of *RB*, Chapter 4.

18. Basil, *The Longer Rules*, 3, in *Ascetical Works*; Augustine, *Ordo Monasterii* 1, in *Augustine of Hippo and His Monastic Rule*. On Basil and Augustine, see also 'Monasticism before Benedict'.

19. See *RB*, Chapters 23–30, 43–6 and 69–71, for guidelines as to discipline and punishment.

20. On the subject of the failure of corporal punishment to bring about good behaviour, see *The Life of St Anselm* by Eadmer (ed. and trans. R. W. Southern (Oxford: Clarendon Press, 1972), pp. 37–8), in which an abbot complains to Anselm (prior and abbot of the Benedictine abbey of Bec, then archbishop of Canterbury 1093–1109) that despite all the beatings they have been given since they were boys his monks are 'stupid brutes'. 'We use every means to force them to get better, but without success,' he says. To which Anselm replies perceptively,

     'You force them? Now tell me, . . . if you plant a tree-shoot in your garden and straightway shut it in on every side so that it has no space to put out its branches, what kind of tree will you have?'
     'A useless one, certainly, with its branches all twisted and knotted.'
     'And whose fault would this be, except your own for shutting it in so unnaturally? Without doubt, this is what you do with your boys. At their oblation they are planted in the garden of the Church, to grow and bring forth fruit for God. But you so terrify them . . . with threats and blows . . . that they doggedly reject everything which could minister to their correction . . . So if you want your boys to be adorned with good habits, you, too, besides the pressure of blows, must apply the encouragement and help of fatherly sympathy and tenderness.'

21. See *RB*, Chapters 22, 30, 37, 39, 45, 54, 59, 63 and 70 for advice on the treatment of children. Chapter 59 discusses the reception of children who are still under-age but gives no rules as to the age at which they could be accepted into the monastery.

22. For Paul of Egypt's conversion to the eremitic life, see Jerome, *Life of Paul*, 4–5 (*ECL* pp. 76–7); for Antony's conversion, see Athanasius, *Life of Antony*, 2, alluding to Matt. 19:21–2 (*ECL* p. 9).

23. Athanasius, *Life of Antony*, 14 (*ECL* p. 19).

24. Polydore Vergil, *De Rerum Inventoribus* (Basle, 1545), 7.1.

25. Palladius, *Lausiac History*, 32.1.

26. Pachomius, *Precepts*, pp. 145–67.

27. These three virtues are often referred to nowadays as the evangeli-

cal counsels or counsels of perfection and are regarded as being at the heart of the monastic life. Benedict however does not mention them explicitly: in *RB* the emphasis is rather on obedience, humility and silence.

28. W. K. L. Clarke, *The Ascetic Works of St Basil* (London: SPCK, 1925), p. 44.

29. Basil, *The Longer Rules* 1–3 and 6–7; Basil's *Shorter Rules* deal with questions of a moral nature.

30. The question of the relations between people of different social status in a monastery occurs also in Jerome's Letter 108 (St Jerome, *Letters and Selected Works*, trans. H. Wace and P. Schaff, in The Nicene and Post-Nicene Fathers of the Christian Church, second series (Oxford: Parker, 1893; reprinted, Edinburgh: T. and T. Clark/Grand Rapids, Michigan: Wm. B. Eerdmans, 1994), vol. 6), where he describes how, in the monastery for women founded by his friend Paula at Bethlehem, the women were divided into three groups for work and meals, according to whether they were noble, middle class or low born, so as to prevent them relapsing into relationships of mistress and servant; within these groups they were all treated equally. However, they all had to dress in the same way and meet together for periods of prayer.

31. Augustine, *Praeceptum* 3, in *Augustine of Hippo and His Monastic Rule*.

32. The Augustinian canons, or canons regular, were priests associated with a cathedral or collegiate church who lived according to a rule; it was in the wake of the reforms of Pope Gregory VII at the end of the eleventh century that many canons adopted St Augustine's Rule. The Premonstratensians belonged to a closed order of monks founded in the early twelfth century in France: their name derives from the Latin *praemonstratum*, meaning '(the place) shown forth', referring to the piece of land granted to them to build a monastery near Laon, which was given the French name Prémontré. The Dominicans formed an order of friars founded in the early thirteenth century: their focus was on preaching and so they are also known as the Order of Preachers.

33. The question of whether a community committed to poverty should live on alms or by the products of manual labour is discussed repeatedly in the history of monasticism, for example among the Franciscans of the thirteenth century.

34. It is from the Latin name (*Collationes*) for Cassian's *Conferences* that the English word 'collation' in its sense 'a light meal' is

derived: as the readings from Cassian's work took place every evening before or after a light supper, the name of the book being read was gradually transferred to the meal itself.

35. Book 5 of Cassian's *Conferences* opens with a list of eight principal vices: gluttony, lust and anger were vices to which those living in a monastic community were particularly prone, while hermits were regarded as likely to succumb to envy, dejection, lethargy, boastfulness and pride. It seems to have been Gregory the Great, in his *Moralia on Job* (31.45; *PL* 76:620–22), who gives us the familiar list of seven deadly sins: pride, anger, envy, greed, sloth, gluttony and lust. On the origins of such lists see Morton W. Bloomfield, *The Seven Deadly Sins* (East Lansing: Michigan State College Press, 1952). (For *PL*, see Notes, p. 109.)

36. Cassian, *Institutes*, 4.39, listed ten rungs on the ladder of humility, leading up to the love that is without fear. It is in Chapter 10 of *RM* that we first find twelve rungs, leading to the same goal, and in this he is followed exactly, if more succinctly, by *RB*, Chapter 7. (For *RM*, see Notes, p. 109.)

37. See *RB 1980* pp. 171–5, on the relationship between *RM* and *RB*.

38. *Chronicle of Monte Cassino* 1 (*Chronica Monasterii Casinensis*, Monumenta Germaniae Historica: Scriptores, 34 (Hanover: Hahn, 1980)). In Geoffrey Chaucer's Prologue to *The Canterbury Tales*, ed. Jill Mann (London: Penguin Books, 2005), l. 173, the monk refers to Maurus' Rule as a synonym for *RB*.

39. Paul the Deacon (*History of the Lombards*, trans. W. D. Foulke (Philadelphia: University of Pennsylvania Press, 2003), 4.17) says that when the monks fled to Rome they took with them a copy of *RB*. This incident is mentioned by Gregory the Great, *Life of Benedict*, 17.2 (*ECL* p. 186), though he does not mention *RB*.

40. On the work of these two men in introducing *RB* into England, see two early eighth-century works: *Life of Wilfrid* by Eddi, Chapter 47; and for Benedict Biscop, *Anonymous History of Abbot Ceolfrid*, 16 (both in *The Age of Bede*, trans. J. F. Webb and D. H. Farmer (Harmondsworth: Penguin Books, 1965; reprinted, 1998)).

41. Matthew Paris recorded these reform measures in his *Chronica Majora*, ed. Luard, 3.499–516.

42. John of Salisbury sent Pope Alexander III a report on the behaviour of this abbot in his Letter 322, dated about 1174 (*The Letters of John of Salisbury*, ed. and trans. W. J. Millor and C. N. L. Brooke (Oxford: Clarendon Press, 1979), vol. 2).

43. Visitation of Godstow nunnery by William, bishop of Lincoln (1432), in the English *Register of Godstow Nunnery*, Early English Text Society, 129 (London: Kegan Paul, 1905), Section 10.

44. Romsey Abbey in Eileen Power, *Medieval English Nunneries* (Cambridge: Cambridge University Press, 1922), p. 307.

45. William Langland, *The Vision of Piers Plowman*, B-text (ed. A. V. C. Schmidt (London: Everyman, 1995), Passus 5, lines 151–63; Chaucer, Prologue, *The Canterbury Tales*, ed. Mann, lines 165–207.

46. On the relevance of *RB* today, see for example *RB 1980*, pp. 141–51.

47. On the importance of silence, see, for example, *RB*, Chapters 4, 6, 7, 38, 42–3, 48–9, 52, and Mayeul de Dreuille, *The Rule of Benedict and the Ascetic Traditions from Asia to the West* (Leominster: Gracewing, 2000), Chapter 7. On humility, see particularly *RB*, Chapter 7.

Further Reading

EDITION

Fry, Timothy, *RB 1980: The Rule of Saint Benedict in Latin and English with Notes* (Collegeville, Minnesota: Liturgical Press, 1981) (referred to as *RB 1980*).

TEXTS FROM THE EARLY PERIOD OF CHRISTIAN MONASTICISM

(In approximate chronological order of composition)

Pachomius, *Precepts*, trans. A. Veilleux, in *Pachomian Koinonia, Vol. 2: Pachomian Chronicles and Rules* (Kalamazoo, Michigan: Cistercian Publications, 1981).

The Lives of the Desert Fathers, trans. Norman Russell (London: Mowbray/Kalamazoo, Michigan: Cistercian Publications, 1981). A translation of the *History of the Monks in Egypt*, which forms Book 2 of the *Vitae Patrum* (*Lives of the Fathers*: *PL* vol. 73). (For *PL*, see Notes, p. 109.)

The Desert Fathers: Sayings of the Early Christian Monks, trans. Benedicta Ward (London: Penguin Books, 2003). A translation of Book 5 of the *Vitae Patrum* (*Lives of the Fathers*: *PL* vol. 73).

Basil, *Ascetical Works*, trans. M. M. Wagner, in *The Fathers of the Church* (Washington D.C.: Catholic University of America Press, 1962), vol. 9.

Early Christian Lives, trans. Carolinne White (London: Penguin Books, 1998). Includes the Lives of Antony, Paul of Thebes, Hilarion, Malchus, Martin of Tours and Benedict (referred to as *ECL*).

Augustine of Hippo and His Monastic Rule, ed. George Lawless (Oxford: Clarendon Press, 1986).

Palladius, *The Lausiac History*, trans. R. T. Meyer, Ancient Christian Writers, 34 (Westminster, Maryland: Newman Press/London: Longman, 1965).

Cassian, John, *Conferences*, trans. Boniface Ramsey, Ancient Christian Writers, 57 (New York/Mahwah, New Jersey: Paulist Press, 1997).

—, *Institutes*, trans. Boniface Ramsey, Ancient Christian Writers, 58 (New York/Mahwah, New Jersey: Newman Press, 2000).

The Rule of the Master, trans. Luke Eberle, with an introduction by Adalbert de Vogüé, Cistercian Studies, 6 (Kalamazoo, Michigan: Cistercian Publications, 1977).

Lanfranc, *The Monastic Constitutions of Lanfranc*, ed. and trans. D. Knowles, rev. edn. C. N. L. Brooke (London: Thomas Nelson, 1951; reprinted, Oxford: Clarendon Press, 2002).

BACKGROUND

Dreuille, Mayeul de, *Seeking the Absolute Love: The Founders of Christian Monasticism* (Leominster: Gracewing/New York: Crossroad, 1999).

Lawrence, C. H., *Medieval Monasticism* (London and New York: Longman, 1984).

Rousseau, Philip, *Ascetics, Authority and the Church in the Age of Jerome and Cassian* (Oxford: Oxford University Press, 1978).

Stenton, F. M., *Anglo-Saxon England* (Oxford: Clarendon Press, 1943), Chapters 5, ('The English Church from Theodore to Boniface') and 13 ('The Tenth-Century Reformation').

Stewart, Columba, *Cassian the Monk* (Oxford and New York: Oxford University Press, 1998).

MODERN INTERPRETATIONS

The Benedictine Handbook (Norwich: Canterbury Press, 2003). Compiled by Benedictines 'for . . . the wider family of the Benedictines'; sections on various aspects of the Rule as it is lived today.

Casey, Michael, *Strangers to the City: Reflections on the Beliefs and Values of the Rule of St. Benedict* (Brewster, Massachusetts: Paraclete Press, 2005).

Derkse, Wil, *The Rule of Benedict for Beginners: Spirituality for Daily Life* (Collegeville, Minnesota: Liturgical Press, 2003). Aimed at those living in a non-monastic context, especially those involved in business management and leadership.

de Waal, Esther, *A Life-giving Way: A Commentary on the Rule of St Benedict* (London and New York: Mowbray 1995). With select bibliography: a personal commentary on the Rule aimed at making it relevant to any individual seeking to lead a profoundly Christian life.

Dreuille, Mayeul de, *The Rule of St Benedict and the Ascetic Traditions from Asia to the West* (Leominster: Gracewing, 2000).

Foster, David, *Reading with God: Lectio divina* (London and New York: Continuum Press, 2005). Helps the reader to study the Bible in the careful and meditative way which Benedict's *lectio divina* is thought to have required.

Henry, Patrick (ed.), *Benedict's Dharma: Buddhists Reflect on the Rule of Benedict* (London: Continuum Press, 2002). On certain aspects of the Benedictine Rule (e.g. discipleship, leadership, tradition) from a non-Christian perspective.

Jamison, Christopher, *Finding Sanctuary: Monastic Steps for Everyday Life* (London: Orion Books, 2007). The Abbot of Worth monastery makes the Rule relevant for those seeking spiritual fulfilment in secular life.

Swan, Laura, *Engaging Benedict: What the Rule Can Teach Us Today* (Notre Dame, Indiana: Ave Maria Press, 2005).

Vogüé, Adalbert de, *Reading St Benedict: Reflections on the Rule*, Cistercian Studies, 151 (Kalamazoo, Michigan: Cistercian Publications, 1994).

Note on the Text

The 'authentic' text in Latin used for this translation is published in Justin McCann's *The Rule of Saint Benedict* (London: Burns Oates, 1952). The history of the text of Benedict's Rule is a fascinating one, but the vast number of manuscripts containing slightly different variations has meant that modern editors have found it hard to agree on the text; however, the differences are usually minor, often amounting only to variations in spelling. The problems can be traced to an early stage when the textual tradition appears to have become divided between the so-called 'authentic' and 'revised' texts. The 'authentic' text is thought to be a witness to the oldest tradition, although the earliest manuscript dates from about 820, now in the Stiftsbibliothek at St Gallen, Switzerland, and known as Sangallensis 914. This is believed to be a copy of a manuscript made for Charlemagne in 787 from another copy that is no longer in existence but which may have been Benedict's own.

The 'revised' text, though not associated directly with Benedict, is found in an earlier manuscript, from about 700, now in the Bodleian Library in Oxford and known as Bodleian Hatton 48. It is probable that it is a version of the Rule made by English monks associated with Wilfrid who assisted in its introduction to England. Benedict's Latin has been revised according to the norms of classical Latinity, sometimes to the point of hypercorrection, e.g. *compraehendant* for *comprehendant* in the Prologue. This version of the Rule was dominant until Charlemagne spread the use of the 'authentic' text which itself was largely superseded by a hybrid version, a mixture of the 'authentic' and 'revised', that became accepted after the tenth cen-

tury. The 'authentic' text has been chosen for this translation
because it is the text most closely associated with Benedict
himself.

Biblical references and translation

In this translation the 150 psalms are numbered according to
English translations of the Bible, which follows that of the
Hebrew Bible. This means that the numbering of Psalms 9–147
will be one ahead of Benedict's Latin text, because the Latin
Bible combined Psalms 9 and 10 and also 114 and 115, but
divided Psalms 116 and 147 into two.

Benedict several times includes citations from books that are
regarded as apocryphal, e.g. the book of Tobit, Sirach (also
known as Ecclesiasticus), and parts of the Book of Daniel.
These were included in the Latin Vulgate but not in the Hebrew
Bible or most English translations.

The translations of biblical passages are my translations of
the text as found in Benedict's Rule. Benedict himself is not
always consistent in giving the text of a passage: for example
in citing Acts 4:35, he once uses *dividebatur* ('was divided', the
word used in the Vulgate version) in Chapter 34 but *dabatur*
in Chapter 55, for what is usually translated as 'was distributed'
in English. Occasionally he does not give what is regarded as
the standard version: for example, in his Prologue, he quotes
John 12:35 as 'Run, while you have the light of life', whereas
most versions have 'walk' instead of 'run'. Such variations
are not uncommon in the works of Benedict's contemporaries.
Benedict did not provide the references for the citations he
quotes or embeds in his text, although he often gives a general
indication of the provenance of a passage, for example, 'as the
Apostle [Paul] says' or 'in accordance with the words of the
prophet'.

A list of abbreviations of those books of the Bible cited by
Benedict and abbreviated in the references in this edition can
be found in the Notes.

In the editorial material, the New Revised Standard Version
is quoted.

Inclusive language

This translation does not use inclusive language because the Benedictine Rule addresses men only.[1] This is not to ignore the tradition of monastic rules written for women dating back to the beginnings of monastic life – Augustine, for example, wrote both a rule for nuns and a 'reprimand for quarrelling nuns'.[2] But both his rule for nuns and the female versions of the Benedictine Rule that appeared in the course of the Middle Ages, were usually versions of the rules for men, with only simple changes of grammatical gender and the substitution of feminine vocabulary where necessary, e.g. 'abbess' for 'abbot' and 'sister' for 'brother'. However, the reform movement within the church in the eleventh century, which inspired a new interest in spirituality and motivated the formation of new monastic orders, seems also to have inspired women to feel a certain dissatisfaction with the content of monastic rules. Robert d' Arbrissel in the late eleventh century provided a brief rule[3] for the women who were to live at the convent he founded at Fontevrault in France, and there exists a version of the Benedictine Rule, possibly dating from the twelfth century, in a manuscript in the British Library in London (MS BL Cotton Claudius D.III) that goes slightly further in its adaptation for women, notably on the subjects of clothing and on the role of priests in the nunnery. And in the early twelfth century Heloise, abbess of the convent of the Paraclete outside Paris, wrote at length to Abelard asking him to write a monastic rule specifically for women, as she felt strongly that Benedict's Rule was not really appropriate for them: indeed, no author of a monastic rule, she alleged, was thinking of women when he wrote, since none contains specific advice on such subjects as women's clothing (for, as she points out, the woollen clothes that men wear are not suitable for menstruating women), or on the question of whether the abbess should dine with visitors as abbots were expected to do. Heloise acknowledges that Benedict did allow a certain amount of discretion and flexibility in his Rule, taking into account the differences between old and young, healthy and sick, and the particular needs of the weaker brothers, but that makes her wonder all the more why he made no specific mention of women's needs.[4] However, any problems regarding details of everyday life as a nun do not prevent the spirituality that grows out of Benedict's blend of the active and contemplative, of the practical and the spiritual, from being applicable to male and female alike.

NOTES

1. For a translation that addresses the *RB* to men and women alike, see, for example, that of Patrick Barry, in *The Benedictine Handbook* (Norwich: Canterbury Press, 2003).
2. Augustine on nuns in *Augustine of Hippo and His Monastic Rule*, ed. George Lawless (Oxford: Clarendon Press, 1986).
3. Robert d'Arbrissel's Rule for women is found in *PL* 162:1079–82. (For *PL*, see Notes p.109.)
4. Heloise to Abelard in Letter 6 (*The Letters of Abelard and Heloise*, trans. Betty Radice, rev. edn. M. T. Clancy (London: Penguin Books, 2003)).

The Rule of Benedict

The Rule of Benedict

Contents

Prologue

Listen, my son, to the master's instructions and take them to heart. These are the instructions of a loving father:[1] receive them gladly and carry them out to good effect so that by the efforts of obedience you may return to him from whom you have withdrawn through the laziness of disobedience. It is to you that my words are now addressed, if you are ready to take up the powerful and glorious weapons of obedience, renouncing your own will with the intention of fighting for the true king, Christ the Lord.

First of all, every time you begin a good work you should pray to him with total commitment to bring it to perfection, so that he who has already been kind enough to count us as his sons will never be disappointed by our doing wrong. We must always obey him with the good things he has given us, so that he never disinherits his children like an angry father or becomes exasperated by our bad behaviour and hands us over to everlasting punishment as a terrifying master does with his delinquent servants, for refusing to follow him to glory.

Now at last we must wake up, as Scripture rouses us to do when it says, 'Now is the time for us to rise from sleep' (Rom. 13:11). Let us open our eyes to the divine light and listen carefully to what the divine voice tells us to do when it cries out each day, 'If you hear his voice today, do not harden your hearts' (Ps. 95:7–8), and also, 'He who has ears to hear, let him listen to what the spirit says to the churches' (Rev. 2:7; see also, Matt. 11:15). And what does he say? 'Come to me, my children and listen to me; I will teach you the fear of the Lord'

7

(Ps. 34:11). 'Run, while you have the light of life, so that the darkness of death does not overtake you' (John 12:35).

The Lord looks for his workman among the crowds of people, and repeatedly calls to him, 'Who is the man who desires life and who wishes to see good days?' (Ps. 34:12). If you hear him and answer, 'I do', God will say to you, 'If you wish to have true and everlasting life, keep your tongue from speaking evil and your lips from speaking deceitfully. Turn away from evil and do good. Seek after peace and pursue it' (Ps. 34:13–14). And when you have done this, my eyes will be upon you and I will listen to your prayers. Even before you call on me, I will say to you, 'Here I am' (Isa. 58:9). What can be sweeter to us, dear brothers, than the Lord's voice when he invites us with these words? Look how the Lord in his loving kindness shows us the way of life.

And so, clothed in faith and the performance of good works, let us set off along his path using the Gospel as our guide, so that we may deserve to see him 'who has called' us 'into his kingdom' (1 Thess. 2:12). If we wish to live in the tabernacle of his kingdom, we will certainly only reach it if we run there by means of good works. But let us question the Lord in the words of the prophet,[2] saying to him, 'Lord, who will live in your tabernacle or who will rest on your holy mountain?' (Ps. 15:1). After putting this question, brothers, we must listen to the Lord's reply for he points out to us the way to this tabernacle. He says, 'He who walks without blemish and who acts justly; he who speaks the truth in his heart and does not use his tongue to deceive; who does not harm his fellow man and does not listen to slander said about him' (Ps. 15:2–3). This person has thwarted the devil in his wickedness by casting him and his suggestion away from the sight of his heart when the devil tries to persuade him to do something: he takes hold of the devil's plans before they have time to mature and dashes them against Christ. Those who fear the Lord and do not allow themselves to become proud because of their good works realize that the good that is in them does not come from their own abilities but from the Lord. They praise the Lord working within them, repeating the words of the prophet, 'Not to us,

Lord, not to us, but to your name give the glory' (Ps. 115:1). In the same way the apostle Paul refused to claim any credit for the success of his preaching, saying, 'By the grace of God I am what I am' (1 Cor. 15:10) and 'The person who boasts should boast in the Lord' (2 Cor. 10:17). That is why the Lord, too, says in the Gospel, 'He who hears these words of mine and acts in accordance with them is like the wise man who built his house on the rock; the floods came, the winds blew and beat upon that house but it did not collapse for it was founded on rock' (Matt. 7:24–5). Having made this pronouncement, the Lord every day expects that we should make our lives conform to this holy advice of his. And so the days of this life are lengthened and we are granted a truce during which to amend our bad ways, as the Apostle[3] says, 'Do you not know that God's patience is leading you to penitence?' (Rom. 2:4). For the Lord in his kindness says, 'I do not want the death of a sinner but that he should be converted and live' (Eze. 33:11). Brothers, we have questioned the Lord about the person who lives in his tabernacle, and we have heard his instructions about living there, but it is for us to fulfil the obligations of those who live there. And so we must prepare our hearts and bodies to fight by means of holy obedience to his instructions. If our natural abilities do not allow us to do something, we must ask the Lord to grant us his grace to assist us. If we wish to escape the punishments of hell and reach eternal life, we must hasten to do now what will profit us forever, while we still have time and while we are in this body and have the opportunity to fulfil all these things by the light of this life.

And so we intend to establish a school[4] for the Lord's service. In doing so we hope to demand nothing that is harsh, nothing oppressive. Even if, in order to maintain a balance, there are some slight restrictions aimed at the correction of errors and the preservation of love, you should not for that reason be frightened off and run away from the path of salvation, which has to be narrow at the beginning. As we make progress in our way of life and in faith, as our heart expands with the inexpressible sweetness of love, we shall run along the path of God's commandments, never abandoning his guidance but persevering in his teaching within the monastery until death, so that we may have a share, through patience, in the sufferings of Christ and thereby also a share in his kingdom. Amen.

I

The kinds of monks

There are clearly four kinds of monks.[1] First there are the coenobites; in other words, those who live in monasteries and do their service under a rule and an abbot. The second are the anchorites, that is, hermits: they are no longer in the first fervour of the monastic life, but have been trained by a lengthy period of probation in the monastery with the support of many others and have learned to fight against the devil. Well-armed, they go out from the ranks of the brothers to the single combat of the desert, without anyone's support; relying on their own strength and with God's help, they are able to fight against physical and mental temptations.

The third and most detestable kind of monks are the sarabaites, who have not been tested like gold in the furnace by any rule and have not learned from experience; instead, softened like lead, they still keep faith with the world in what they do. Their tonsure makes it clear that they are lying to God. In groups of two or three or even singly, without a shepherd, enclosed not in the Lord's sheepfold but in their own, they take their own desires and pleasures as their laws, calling their every whim holy and claiming that whatever they do not want to do is unlawful.

The fourth kind of monks are known as gyrovagues: they spend their whole lives wandering around different regions, staying in different cells for three or four days at a time, always moving from one place to another and never remaining in the same place, indulging their own desires and caught in the snares of greed. They are in every way worse than the sarabaites. It is better to say nothing than to speak about all of them and their despicable way of life. And so, leaving them aside, let us proceed with God's help to make provision for the coenobites who are the most effective kind of monks.

2

What kind of man the abbot should be

To be worthy of being in charge of a monastery, the abbot must always bear in mind what his title signifies and live up to the name of 'superior'. For he is believed to be Christ's representative in the monastery, since his title is one that is applied to Christ, as is clear from the Apostle's words, 'You have received the spirit of adoption of sons by which we call out, Abba,[1] Father' (Rom. 8:15). And so the abbot should not teach or decree or command anything contrary to the Lord's instructions; instead, he should work into the minds of his disciples the Lord's commands and his teaching, as if they were the yeast of divine justice. The abbot must never forget that at the dread judgement of God he will have to give an account of his teaching and of his disciples' obedience. The abbot must be aware that the shepherd will bear the blame for whatever deficiencies the sheep's owner might find in them. However, if the shepherd has focused all his efforts on his restless and disobedient flock and been very careful to correct their bad behaviour, then he will be acquitted at the Lord's judgement and will say to the Lord in the words of the prophet, 'I have not hidden your justice in my heart; I have spoken your truth and your salvation (Ps. 40:10); but they have despised and rejected me' (Isa. 1:2). And so in the end the disobedient sheep entrusted to his care will be punished by a devastating death.

Consequently, when someone is appointed abbot he should manage his disciples by teaching them in two ways: he ought to display all that is good and holy in his actions as much as in his words. In this way he will use words to teach the more able disciples the commands of the Lord, while to those who are

stubborn and less intellectually sophisticated, he will demonstrate the Lord's teaching by means of his own actions. He
should indicate by his actions that everything he tells his disciples
to be against the Lord's teaching is to be avoided, so that he is not
found guilty of failing to practise what he preaches, and so that
God never says to him in his sin, 'Why do you repeat my just
commands and boast of my covenant with your mouth? You
have hated discipline and have thrown my words behind you'
(Ps. 50:16–17), or 'You saw the speck in your brother's eye but
you failed to see the beam in your own' (Matt. 7:3). He must
not show any favouritism in the monastery. He ought not to
love one more than another, unless he finds one to be better in
good deeds and in obedience. A person who is born free should
not be accorded higher status than one who was a slave, unless
other reasonable grounds exist for this. If the abbot considers
it right, he can make alterations to anyone's status, when justice
so demands. Otherwise the brothers should keep to their regular
positions, because we are all one in Christ, whether slave or
free, and we are soldiers of the same rank fighting under the
one Lord, 'for God shows no partiality' (Rom. 2:11). The only
way in which we are distinguished in his sight is if we are found
to be better than others in good works and in humility. The
abbot should therefore love all equally and apply the same
discipline to all, according to what they deserve.

In his teaching the abbot must always observe the Apostle's
advice when he says, 'Reprove, appeal, rebuke' (2 Tim. 4:2). In
other words the abbot must adapt himself to different circumstances, combining encouragement with threats, displaying the
sternness of a teacher and the kind affection of a father. This
means that he should rebuke more sternly those who are undisciplined and restless, and appeal to those who are obedient,
mild and patient to make even more progress. We advise him
to rebuke and to punish those who are careless and contemptuous. He must not ignore the faults of those who do wrong,
but as far as possible he should cut such faults out at the root
as soon as they appear, remembering the fate of Eli,[2] priest of
Shiloh. On the first and second occasions, he should use a verbal
rebuke to reprimand those who are decent and reasonable, but

those who are wicked and obstinate, arrogant or disobedient he should restrain by means of a beating and corporal punishment, as soon as they start to go wrong, remembering that it is written, 'The fool cannot be corrected by words' (Prov. 18:2), and again 'Beat your son with the rod and you will save his soul from death' (Prov. 23:14).

The abbot should always remember what he is and what his title signifies, and should bear in mind that more will be demanded from the person to whom more has been entrusted (Luke 12:48). He should also be aware that it is a difficult and demanding task to guide souls and to manage many different temperaments, using encouragement to deal with one person, rebuke with another, persuasion with a third, according to the disposition and understanding of each one. He must adapt himself to all in such a way that he does not lose any of the flock entrusted to him, but may even rejoice to find that his flock is a good one and that it has increased in number.

Above all let him be careful not to show too much concern for trivial matters, for what is earthly and temporary, neglecting the salvation of the souls entrusted to him or failing to accord sufficient importance to it. He should always remember that he has received these souls so that he may guide them and that he will have to give an account of them. To prevent him perhaps complaining about a lack of resources, let him remember that it is written, 'First seek the kingdom of God and his justice and all these things will be added to you' (Matt. 6:33), and again, 'Those who fear him lack nothing' (Ps. 34:9). The abbot must bear in mind that the person who receives souls for guidance should be ready to give an account of them. He should be aware that however many brothers he has under his care, on the Day of Judgement he will definitely have to give an account to the Lord of each of their souls, and indeed of his own soul, too. And so, fearing always the future interrogation that the shepherd will have to undergo regarding the sheep entrusted to him and anxious about the account he must give of others, he will think carefully about the account he must give of himself. In this way, as he helps to correct others by reprimanding them, he will find that his own faults are corrected.

3

Summoning the brothers for consultation

Whenever any important matters need to be dealt with in the monastery, the abbot should gather the whole community together and set out the agenda in person. When he has listened to the brothers' advice, he should consider it carefully and then do what he decides is best. We have said that everybody should be summoned to take part in the discussion because the Lord often reveals the better course to a younger person. Let the brothers offer their advice with all deference and humility and not venture to defend their own views obstinately. It is up to the abbot to decide what he thinks is the best course, and then the others must accept this. Nevertheless, just as it is proper for disciples to obey their master, so it is right that he should arrange everything wisely and justly.

Everyone should take the rule as his guide in all circumstances; no one must deviate from it rashly. Let no one in the monastery follow the wishes of his own heart or venture to dispute with the abbot defiantly or outside the monastery in public. If anyone does, he should be subjected to the discipline of the rule. However, the abbot himself must be guided by fear of God and observe the rule in all his actions, aware that he will certainly have to give an account to God, the most just judge, regarding each decision he makes.

If matters of lesser importance need to be dealt with for the good of the monastery, the abbot need only consult the older brothers, in accordance with the words of Scripture: 'Do everything with counsel and when it is done you will not regret it' (Sir. 32:24).

4

The tools for good works

First of all, 'love the Lord God with all your heart, with all your soul and with all your strength', then 'love your neighbour as yourself' (Matt. 22:37, 39; Mark 12:30–31; Luke 10:27).

'Do not kill, do not commit adultery, do not steal or covet, do not give false evidence about each other' (Rom. 13:9). 'Honour all men' (1 Pet. 2:17) and 'do not do to someone else what you do not want done to you' (Tob. 4:15). 'Deny yourself so as to follow Christ' (Matt. 16:24; Luke 9:23), 'discipline the body' (1 Cor. 9:27) and do not be self-indulgent; put a high value on fasting. Relieve the poor, clothe those who are in need of clothing, visit the sick and bury the dead; help those in trouble and console those who grieve. Do not be guided in your actions by the values of this world, and do not value anything more highly than the love of Christ.

Do not act in anger or harbour a grudge. Do not allow deceit to lurk in your heart, and do not make peace if it is not genuine. Do not abandon love. Do not swear, in case you perjure yourself. Speak the truth from heart and mouth. 'Do not repay one wrong with another' (1 Thess. 5:15; 1 Pet. 3:9). Do not do wrong to anyone but bear patiently any wrongs done to you. 'Love your enemies' (Matt. 5:44; Luke 6:27). Do not repay insults with insults but rather with kind words. Endure persecution for the sake of justice (Matt. 5:10). 'Do not be arrogant or drunken' (Titus 1:7) or greedy. Do not be lazy or a grumbler. Do not cast aspersions on others. Put your hope in God. If you notice anything good in yourself, give the credit to God, not to yourself. Be aware that the wrongs you commit are always your own and admit to them.

Fear the Day of Judgement and be terrified of hell. Long for eternal life with all your spiritual desire. Each day remind yourself of your mortality. Keep a watch on the actions of your life at all times. Be aware that God can certainly see you wherever you are. As soon as wicked thoughts spring into your heart, dash them against Christ. Guard your mouth from all wicked or warped words. Do not take pleasure in talking a lot. Do not say foolish things or things that are intended to cause laughter. Do not take pleasure in excessive or unrestrained laughter. Enjoy listening to holy readings. Pray frequently. Confess your past sins to God each day in prayer with tears and sighs. Correct your faults for the future. 'Do not indulge the desires of the flesh' (Gal. 5:16). Hate your own will. Obey the abbot's commands in all circumstances, even if he (which God forbid) does not act in accordance with them. Remember the Lord's words, 'Do what they say and not what they do' (Matt. 23:3). Do not strive to be referred to as holy before you are so: be holy first, so that you may more accurately be referred to as holy.

Carry out God's commandments in what you do every day. Embrace chastity. Hate no one. Do not be jealous or give in to feelings of envy. Do not take pleasure in disputes. Avoid pride, respect your elders and care for those younger than yourself. Pray for your enemies in the love of Christ. Before the day's end be reconciled with anyone with whom you have a disagreement. Never despair of God's mercy.

These, then, are the tools of the spiritual craft. If we use them without ceasing, day and night, and if we return them on the Day of Judgement, the Lord will reward us as he himself has promised: 'what the eye has not seen nor the ear heard, God has prepared for those who love him' (1 Cor. 2:9). The workshop where we diligently work at all these tasks is the enclosure of the monastery, in the stability of the community.

5

Obedience

The first step towards humility is unhesitating obedience, which comes naturally to all who hold Christ dearer than anything else. As soon as the superior gives an order, they carry it out as promptly as if the order came from God, either because of the holy service they have promised to perform, or because they are afraid of hell, or for the sake of the glory of eternal life. The Lord says of such people, 'He obeyed me as soon as he heard me' (Ps. 18:44). And again he says to the teachers, 'Anyone who listens to you listens to me' (Luke 10:16). Such people immediately abandon their own concerns and give up their own will. They stop what they are doing, leaving it unfinished; with obedient steps they turn words into deeds, following the voice of the one who gives the order. The master's order and the disciple's perfect fulfilment of it occur more or less simultaneously. Those who are motivated by a desire to progress towards eternal life carry out both promptly, in the fear of the Lord. They hasten along the narrow way, according to the Lord's words, 'Narrow is the way that leads to life' (Matt. 7:14). They do not live according to their own wishes or indulge their own desires and pleasures, but progress according to someone else's judgement and orders, living in monasteries and choosing to have an abbot in charge of them. Such people undoubtedly conform to the saying of the Lord where he says, 'I have not come to do my own will but that of him who sent me' (John 6:38).

But this very obedience will be acceptable to God and pleasing to men only if the order given is carried out without hesitation, without delay, without apathy, without complaint and without any answering back from the one who is unwilling. The obedience offered to the superiors is in fact shown to God, for he himself said, 'Anyone who listens to you listens to me' (Luke 10:16). The disciples ought to offer it with a good will because 'God loves a cheerful giver' (2 Cor. 9:7). For if the disciple obeys with resentment and grumbles not just with his lips but also in his heart, even if he carries out the order, it will still not be acceptable to God who sees that his heart is complaining. As a result he will receive no reward – in fact unless he changes for the better, he will incur the penalty due to those who grumble.

6

Restraint of speech

Let us do as the prophet says: 'I said, I will keep a watch over my ways so that I do not offend with my tongue; I have put a guard on my mouth . . . I have kept silent and I was humbled and I refrained from speaking good things' (Ps. 39:1–2). Here the prophet shows that if it is occasionally right to refrain from saying good things because one values silence, there is all the more reason to refrain from saying bad things because sin will be punished. In fact silence is so important that permission to speak should rarely be granted even to disciples who have made much spiritual progress, however good and holy and constructive their words might be. For it says in Scripture, 'You will not escape sin if you talk too much' (Prov. 10:19), and in another passage, 'The tongue has power over life and death' (Prov. 18:21). It is right that the master should speak and teach while the disciple should be silent and listen.

And so, if something needs to be requested from a superior,[1] the request should be made with all humility and submissive respect. We condemn jokes and idle gossip and anything said to make others laugh, and we ban such things from all places: the disciple is not allowed to open his mouth to say things of this kind.

7

Humility

Holy Scripture calls to us, brothers, saying, 'Anyone who exalts himself will be humbled and anyone who humbles himself will be exalted' (Luke 14:11). It thereby shows us that all exaltation is a form of pride, and the prophet indicates that he takes care to avoid this when he says, 'Lord, my heart is not exalted and my eyes are not raised up. I have not walked among the great nor sought after wonderful things beyond my reach.' But why? 'If I did not have a humble spirit or if I exalted my soul, then you would punish my soul like a baby weaned from its mother' (Ps. 131:1, 2).

And so, my brothers, if we wish to reach the highest peak of humility and if we wish to attain quickly that heavenly exaltation towards which we climb by means of the humility of this life, we must set up for our ascent the ladder that Jacob saw in his dream, on which the angels appeared to him, descending and ascending.[1] For we should surely interpret their descent and ascent as referring to the descent we make by self-exaltation and the ascent by humility. That ladder is our life in this world which God raises to heaven if we are humble in heart. Our body and soul form the sides of this ladder into which the divine calling has fixed the different rungs of humility and discipline which we have to climb.

The first step towards humility is to keep the fear of God in mind at all times. There must be absolutely no room for forgetfulness, and one must always remember everything that God has commanded. Do not forget that those who are scornful of God will burn in hell for their sins. Keep in mind the eternal life that God has prepared for those who fear him. Guard yourself at all times from sins and vices, whether of thought or speech or hands or feet or of self-will, as well as of desire of the body. Remember that God is watching you from heaven at every moment, and that wherever you are your actions can be seen by the Divine Being and are being reported by the angels at all times. The prophet teaches us this when he shows that God is always present in our thoughts, 'God searches the mind and tests the heart' (Ps. 7:9), he says, and similarly, 'The Lord knows the thoughts of men' (Ps. 94:11). He also says, 'You have understood my thoughts from afar' (Ps. 139:2), and 'A man's thought will confess to you.'[2] To guard against bad thoughts, the good brother should constantly repeat in his heart, 'If I keep myself from wickedness, then I will be perfect in his sight' (Ps. 18:23).

We are forbidden to do our own will, for Scripture says to us, 'Turn away from your own will' (Sir. 18:30). Similarly in the Lord's Prayer we ask God that his will be done in us (Matt. 6:10). It is right that we are taught not to do our own will since we are afraid of that saying of Scripture, 'There are ways that seem straight to men but which lead down to the depths of hell' (Prov. 16:25), and we also tremble at what is said of those who fail to take notice, 'They are corrupt and have become abominable in their pleasures' (Ps. 14:1).

As to desire of the body we must believe that God is always present to us, since the prophet says to the Lord, 'Every desire of mine is before your eyes' (Ps. 38:9). One must, therefore, beware of evil desire because death lies in wait at the gateway to pleasure. And so Scripture gives us the following command, 'Do not pursue your lusts' (Sir. 18:30). And so, if 'the eyes of the Lord watch over both good and bad' (Prov. 15:3), and the Lord always 'looks down from heaven on the sons of men to see if there is anyone who understands and seeks God' (Ps. 14:2), and if the results of our actions are reported to the Lord, throughout the day and night, by angels assigned to us, we must be careful at all times, my brothers, that God does not see us at any time turning towards wrongdoing and becoming worthless, in the words of the prophet in the psalm (Ps. 14:3). He might spare us for the moment because he is loving and waits for us to turn to the better, but he will say to us in the future, 'You did this and I was silent' (Ps. 50:21).

The second step towards humility is not to love your own will and not to take pleasure in satisfying your own desires. Instead, imitate in your actions the voice of the Lord when he says, 'I have not come to do my will but that of the one who sent me' (John 6:38). And again Scripture says, 'Self-indulgence has its own punishment and necessity wins the prize.'[3]

The third step towards humility is to submit to your superior with complete obedience out of love for God, imitating the Lord of whom the Apostle says, 'He was made obedient even to the point of death' (Phil. 2:8).

The fourth step towards humility is to cling to patience with equanimity, practising obedience when you encounter painful and difficult experiences and even unjust treatment. You should endure all this without growing angry or running away, for Scripture says, 'He who stands firm right until the end will be saved' (Matt. 10:22), and similarly, 'Let your heart be comforted and wait for the Lord' (Ps. 27:14). To indicate that the person who is faithful ought to endure all things, however difficult, for the Lord's sake, Scripture says in the person of those who suffer, 'For your sake we face death all day. We are regarded as lambs for the slaughter' (Rom. 8:36). Confident in their hope of divine reward, they go forward with joy, saying, 'But in all these things we are victorious because of him who loved us' (Rom. 8:37). Similarly in another passage of Scripture, 'You have tested us, Lord; you have tried us in the fire; you have led us into a snare; you have laid troubles on our back' (Ps. 66:10–11). And to show that we ought to live under the guidance of a prior, it goes on to say, 'You have set men over our heads' (Ps. 66:12). Carrying out the Lord's commands in adversity and persecution, when struck on one cheek they offer the other, when someone takes their tunic they offer their cloak as well, when forced to walk a mile, they walk two, and they join the Apostle Paul in 'putting up with false brothers' (2 Cor. 11:26) and 'blessing those who curse them' (1 Cor. 4:12).

The fifth step towards humility is to confess humbly to the abbot all the wicked thoughts that spring to mind and anything you have secretly done wrong, as Scripture encourages us to do when it says, 'Reveal to the Lord your path and put your hope in him' (Ps. 37:5). Similarly it says, 'Confess to the Lord for he is good and his mercy lasts forever' (Ps. 106: 1). As the prophet says, 'I have revealed to you my faults and I have not concealed the unjust things I have done. I said, I will accuse myself of my wrongs to the Lord and you forgave the wickedness of my heart' (Ps. 32:5).

The sixth step towards humility is for the monk to be content with the lowest position and most menial treatment, and to consider himself incompetent and worthless with regard to everything he is told to do, saying to himself in the words of the prophet, 'I have been reduced to nothing and I know nothing. I am regarded as a beast of burden in your eyes; yet I am always with you' (Ps. 73:22–3).

The seventh step towards humility is for him not only to claim that he is beneath everyone else and worse than them, but also to be convinced of this deep in his heart, humbling himself and saying with the prophet, 'I am a worm and not a man, hated by others and a laughing-stock to the people' (Ps. 22:6). 'I have been raised up and then humiliated and thrown into confusion' (Ps. 88:15), and also 'It is good for me that you have humiliated me so that I might learn your commandments' (Ps. 119:71).

The eighth step towards humility is for the monk to do only what is commended by the common rule of the monastery and the example of his superiors.

The ninth step towards humility is for the monk to keep his tongue in check and to refrain from speaking. He should only speak when questioned, as Scripture demonstrates for 'you will not escape sin if you talk too much' (Prov. 10:19) and 'a talkative man loses his way on earth' (Ps. 140:11).

The tenth step towards humility is to avoid being easily provoked to laughter, for it says in Scripture that 'the person who raises his voice in laughter is a fool' (Sir. 21:20).

The eleventh step towards humility is for the monk to speak gently and without laughter, but with humility and seriousness, saying only a few, reasonable words, and not speaking in a loud voice, for as it is written, 'The wise man is recognized by his few words.'[4]

The twelfth step towards humility is for the monk always to display humility, both in his attitude and his behaviour, to those who see him. In other words, in the work of God,[5] in the oratory, in the monastery, in the garden, on the road, in the fields, or anywhere else, whether sitting, walking or standing, he should always have his head bent, his eyes fixed on the ground, regarding himself at all times as guilty of his sins, and imagining that he is already appearing before the dread judgement. He should constantly repeat to himself in his heart the words of the publican in the Gospels who said, with his eyes fixed on the ground, 'Lord, I am a sinner and not worthy to raise my eyes to heaven' (Luke 18:13), and also the words of the prophet, 'I am bowed down and utterly humiliated' (Ps. 38:6).

When the monk has climbed up all these steps of humility, he will reach 'the perfect love of God which casts out all fear' (1 John 4:18). As a result, all the things he did out of fear he will begin to perform without effort, out of habit and naturally, no longer out of the fear of hell but as a good habit out of the love of Christ and delight in virtue. The Lord in his kindness will by the Holy Spirit give evidence of this in his workman, now cleansed from vices and sins.

8

The divine office at night

In winter, in other words from the first of November until Easter, it seems reasonable for the monks to rise at the eighth hour of the night[1] so that they may rest until a little after midnight and rise with their food fully digested. In the time remaining after the night office, those brothers who need to should study the psalms and lessons. From Easter to November, the hour of rising should be set in such a way that there is only a very short interval after the night office,[2] when the brothers can go out to deal with nature's needs; this will be followed at once by Lauds which should be said at daybreak.

9

The number of psalms to be said at the night office

In winter the office should begin with the verse,[1] 'Lord, open my lips, and my mouth will show forth your praise' (Ps. 51:15) repeated three times. There should then follow Psalm 3 and the Gloria,[2] then Psalm 95, which should be chanted, preferably with an antiphon.[3] That should be followed by one of the Ambrosian hymns,[4] then six psalms with their antiphons. After these, once the verse has been said the abbot should give a blessing. When everyone is seated in their places, the brothers should take it in turns to read aloud three readings from the book on the lectern, and between the readings three responsories[5] should be chanted. Two of the responsories should be said without the Gloria, but after the third reading the reader should chant the Gloria. As soon as he begins to chant it, all should rise from their seats at once out of honour and respect for the Holy Trinity. The books to be read at the night office are those which have divine authority, both from the Old and the New Testaments, but also the commentaries on them that were written by recognized and orthodox catholic[6] fathers. After these three readings with their responsories, there should follow the remaining six psalms to be sung with the Alleluia.[7] These are followed by a reading from the Apostle to be recited by heart, the verse and the petition of the litany, that is the Kyrie Eleison.[8] This brings the night office to a close.

10

Arrangements for the night office in summer

From Easter to 1 November[1] the number of psalms should be kept as prescribed in the previous section, except that there should be no readings from the book because the nights are so short. Instead of the three readings, there should just be one from the Old Testament, said by heart, followed by a short responsory. Everything else should be done in the manner prescribed; in other words, there should never be fewer than twelve psalms said during the night office, in addition to Psalms 3 and 95.

The night office on Sundays

On Sundays the brothers should rise earlier for the night office for which the following arrangements apply. When the six psalms and the verse have been chanted (as prescribed in a previous chapter) and everyone is duly sitting in their stalls in the correct order, the four readings with their responsories should be read out from the book as we stated earlier. Only with the fourth responsory should the reader chant the Gloria. As soon as he begins everyone should stand up out of respect. After these readings the remaining six psalms should follow in order, together with their antiphons (as in the case of the earlier ones), and a verse. Then another four readings should be read with their responsories, in the same order as above. After this there should be three canticles from the prophets,[1] as decided by the abbot, and these should be chanted with the Alleluia. When the verse has been said and the abbot has given the blessing, another four readings from the New Testament should be read, in the same order as above. After the fourth responsory the abbot should begin the hymn *Te Deum laudamus*.[2] When this has been sung right through, the abbot should read the lesson from the Gospel while everyone stands out of reverence and fear. At the end of the reading everyone should respond 'Amen'. Then the abbot should immediately follow with the hymn *Te decet laus*, and after he has given the blessing Lauds should begin.

This order for the night office should be kept on Sundays all the year round both in summer and winter, unless the monks happen to be a bit late getting up (which God forbid) and have to shorten the readings or responsories in some way. Great care must be taken that this does not happen, but if it does, then the one whose carelessness was responsible must make amends to God in the oratory.

12

The office of Lauds

On Sundays Lauds should begin with Psalm 67, chanted straight through without the antiphon. After this Psalm 51 should be said, with the Alleluia, and then Psalms 118 and 63. Then the Benedicite[1] and Psalms 148 to 150,[2] followed by a reading from Revelation to be recited by heart together with the responsory, an Ambrosian hymn, a verse, a canticle from the Gospel,[3] and finally the Kyrie Eleison.

13

Arrangements for Lauds on ordinary days

On ordinary days the office of Lauds should be celebrated as follows: Psalm 67 should be said without an antiphon and quite slowly as on Sundays, to give everyone a chance to arrive in time for Psalm 51, which should be said with an antiphon. After this, two more psalms should be said according to custom: in other words, on Mondays Psalms 5 and 36, on Tuesdays Psalms 43 and 57, on Wednesdays Psalms 64 and 65, on Thursdays Psalms 88 and 90, on Fridays Psalms 76 and 92, on Saturdays Psalm 143 together with the canticle from Deuteronomy[1] which should be divided into two with separate Glorias. On other days a canticle from the prophets should be said on the appropriate day according to the custom of the Roman church. These should be followed by Psalms 148 to 150, and then a reading from the Apostle should be recited by heart, followed by the responsory, an Ambrosian hymn, a verse, a canticle from the Gospel, and finally the Kyrie Eleison.

Of course the offices of Lauds and Vespers must never be concluded without a recitation by a superior of the whole of the Lord's Prayer (Matt. 6:9–13) at the end for everyone to listen to, to prevent the thorns of resentment springing up, as they so easily do. For if the monks are confronted by the pledge made in this prayer when they say, 'Forgive us as we forgive' (Matt. 6:12), it is to be hoped that they will cleanse themselves from this type of sin. At other times only the final part[2] of that prayer should be said to allow everyone to make the response, 'But deliver us from evil' (Matt. 6:13).

14

Arrangements for the night office on saints' days

On saints' days and on all feast-days, the office should be performed in the same way as is prescribed for Sundays, except that the psalms or antiphons or readings appropriate for that day should be said; but the general arrangement remains the same as indicated earlier.

15

The times for saying the Alleluia

From the holy feast of Easter until Pentecost, the Alleluia should always be said both with the psalms and the responsories. From Pentecost until the beginning of Lent, it should be said every night only with the last six psalms at the night office. Every Sunday outside Lent, the canticles at Lauds, Prime, Terce, Sext and None[1] should be said with the Alleluia, but at Vespers with an antiphon. The responsories should never be said with the Alleluia, except between Easter and Pentecost.

16

Arrangements for the divine office during the day

The prophet says, 'Seven times a day have I praised you' (Ps. 119:164). We will fulfil this sacred number seven if we perform the duties of our service at the hours of Lauds, Prime, Terce, Sext, None, Vespers and Compline, because it was with reference to these hours of the day that he said, 'Seven times a day have I praised you.' With regard to the night office the same prophet says, 'In the middle of the night I rose to praise you' (Ps. 119:62). At these times, then, we should give praise to our creator 'for his just judgements' (Ps. 119:164); in other words, at Lauds, Prime, Terce, Sext, None, Vespers and Compline; and let us rise to praise him also at night.

17

The number of psalms to be said at these hours

We have already established the order in which to say the psalms at the night office and Lauds. Now we must consider the remaining offices. At Prime three psalms should be said, one by one, each with a separate Gloria; and before the psalms begin, the hymn for that office should be sung after the verse 'God, come to my assistance'[1] (Ps. 70:1). After these three psalms, there should be a reading, a verse and the Kyrie Eleison, followed by the dismissal. At Terce, Sext and None, the prayers are to be said in the same way; in other words, the verse, the hymn appropriate for each of the offices, three psalms, a reading and another verse, the Kyrie Eleison, and the dismissal. If there is a large congregation, the antiphons should be said as well, but if it is small, the psalms should be sung straight through.

The service of Vespers should be limited to four psalms and their antiphons. After these psalms a lesson should be read, then the responsory, an Ambrosian hymn, a verse, a canticle from the Gospel, the Kyrie Eleison, and finally the Lord's Prayer. Compline should be limited to three psalms to be said straight through without an antiphon. After these there should be a hymn appropriate for that hour, a reading, a verse, the Kyrie Eleison and a blessing to finish with.

18

The order of the psalms

First of all the monks should say the verse, 'God, come to my assistance; Lord, hasten to help me' (Ps. 70:1), followed by the Gloria and the hymn proper to each hour. Then, at Prime on Sundays, four sections of Psalm 119 should be said; at each of the remaining hours (in other words at Terce, Sext and None), three sections of this same Psalm 119 should be said. At Prime on Mondays, let three psalms, namely Psalms 1, 2 and 6 be said. Similarly at Prime every day until Sunday, they should say three psalms in order as far as Psalm 20, remembering to divide Psalm 9 and Psalm 18 in two. In this way the night office on Sundays will always start with Psalm 21.

At Terce, Sext and None on Mondays, let the remaining nine sections of Psalm 119 be said, three at each of these hours. When Psalm 119 has been said over two days, that is on Sunday and Monday, three psalms should be said at Terce, at Sext and at None on Tuesdays from Psalms 120 to 128, in other words nine psalms in all. They should always repeat these psalms at the same hours every day until Sunday, while the order of the hymns, readings and verses should be the same every day. In this way Psalm 119 will always begin on Sundays.

Every day four psalms should be sung during Vespers. These should start with Psalm 110 and go on to Psalm 147, leaving out those that are reserved for special hours, in other words Psalms 118 to 128, 134, and 143; all the other psalms should be said at Vespers. And since there are three psalms too few, those from this sequence that seem rather long should be divided, in other words Psalms 139, 144 and 145. But because Psalm 117 is short it should be joined on to Psalm 116.

Now that the order of psalms at Vespers has been established, the rest (namely the reading, responsory, hymn, verse and canticle) should be carried out in the order prescribed in the previous chapter.

At Compline each day the same psalms should be repeated, namely Psalms 4, 91 and 133.[1]

Now that the order of the psalms for the daytime offices has been explained, all the remaining psalms should be distributed equally over the seven night offices, by dividing the longer psalms and assigning twelve psalms to each night of the week. But we strongly recommend that if anyone finds this arrangement unacceptable, he should rearrange them if he can think of a better order, as long as he makes sure that every week the whole psalter with its 150 psalms is recited in full and that the whole sequence always starts from the beginning at the night office on Sundays. For it is clear that monks are too lazy in the service of their devotion if they sing less than the whole psalter with the customary canticles in the course of a week: after all, we read that our holy predecessors had the energy to perform in a single day what we, with our lukewarm faith, aspire to carry out in the course of a whole week.[2]

19

Regulations regarding the singing of psalms

We believe that God is present everywhere and that the eyes of the Lord watch the good and the bad in every place, but we should believe that this is especially true when we are celebrating the divine office. And so we must always bear in mind the words of the prophet when he says, 'Serve the Lord in fear' (Ps. 2:11), 'sing wisely' (Ps. 47:7) and 'in the sight of the angels I will sing to you' (Ps. 138:1). Let us then consider carefully how we ought to behave in the sight of God and his angels, and let us stand to sing in such a way that there is no discrepancy between our thoughts and the words we are singing.

20

Reverence in prayer

If we wish to ask a favour of a powerful person, we would not dare to do so except with humility and respect. Is it not all the more important for us to pray to the Lord, the God of all, with the utmost humility and purity of devotion? We must be aware that he will only listen to us if we pray not so much at length but with purity of heart and tears of compunction. And so our prayer should be kept short and simple, unless divine grace inspires us to prolong our prayer. In community, however, prayer should be kept very short, and when a superior gives the signal everybody should stand at the same time.

2 I

The deans of the monastery

If the community is quite large, brothers of good repute and a holy way of life should be chosen and appointed as deans to be responsible in all matters for the ten monks in their charge, in obedience to God's commandments and the abbot's orders. The deans should be selected as being those with whom the abbot can confidently share his burdens; they should not be chosen because of their rank in the community but for their virtuous behaviour, their learning and wisdom. If any dean is found to be puffed up with pride and deserves to be rebuked, he should be reprimanded once, twice and even a third time; if he still refuses to correct his attitude, he should be demoted from office and replaced by someone worthy of it. We advise that similar measures be taken in the case of the prior.

22

Sleeping arrangements

The monks should sleep in separate beds, and they should be given bedding appropriate to their way of life, as the abbot decides. If possible they should all sleep in one room but if there are too many of them, then they should sleep in groups of ten or twenty under the supervision of older monks. A candle must be left burning all night in the room until morning. The monks should sleep clothed and wearing a belt or cord round their waist but should not have their knives at their sides while they are sleeping, in case they accidentally cut themselves in their sleep. If they sleep with their clothes on, the monks will always be ready, and when the signal is given, they will get up without delay and hurry to reach the work of God before the others, but with the utmost seriousness and restraint. The younger brothers' beds must not be next to each other but interspersed among those of the older monks. When the brothers get up to go to the work of God, they should encourage each other gently, for those who are sleepy often try to make excuses.

23

Excommunication for offences

If a brother is found to be insubordinate, disobedient, arrogant, complaining or in any way uncooperative and contemptuous of the holy rule and the orders of his superiors, he should be rebuked by his elders once or twice, in private, as the Lord advised (Matt. 18:15). But if he does not correct his ways, he must be reprimanded publicly in front of everyone. If even then his behaviour does not improve, he must be excommunicated,[1] provided that he understands the seriousness of this punishment. But if he persists in error, he should undergo corporal punishment.

24

Degrees of excommunication

The severity of the excommunication or punishment meted out should be in proportion to the seriousness of the fault, and it is for the abbot to judge this. If a brother is found guilty of a minor offence, he should be excluded from the communal meal. Anyone forbidden to share in the meal must follow this rule: in the oratory he is not allowed to lead a psalm or antiphon or to read the lesson until he has made amends. He must eat his meal alone after the other brothers have finished theirs, so that if, for example, the brothers eat at the sixth hour, this brother must eat at the ninth; if the brothers eat at the ninth hour, he should eat in the evening; and this regime should continue until he has made sufficient amends and been pardoned.

25

Serious offences

The brother who is guilty of a more serious fault should be excluded both from the meal and the oratory. No other brother is allowed to associate with him or talk to him. He must work alone at the task set him, continuing in sorrow and repentance, meditating on those terrifying words spoken by the Apostle, 'This person is to be handed over for the destruction of the flesh so that his spirit may be saved on the day of the Lord' (1 Cor. 5:5). He should eat his meals alone, and it is up to the abbot to decide how much food and at what time it is suitable for him to eat. No one passing by should give either him or his food a blessing.

26

Unauthorized association with the
excommunicated

If a brother dares to associate in any way with an excommunicated brother, to speak to him or give him a message without being told to do so by the abbot, he should receive exactly the same punishment of excommunication.

27

The abbot's care for the excommunicated

The abbot should show the utmost care and concern for those brothers who have done wrong 'for it is not healthy people who need a doctor but those who are sick' (Matt. 9:12). And so, like an experienced doctor, he should try every possible remedy. He should send in 'senpectae',[1] in other words, older and experienced brothers who can console the troubled brother in private, as it were, encouraging him to give humble satisfaction and comforting him 'so that he is not overwhelmed by excessive sorrow' (2 Cor. 2:7); instead, 'let love be strengthened in him' (2 Cor. 2:8) as the Apostle says, and let everyone pray for him.

The abbot should exercise great care and extreme sensitivity, making every effort not to lose any of the sheep entrusted to him. He must bear in mind that he has undertaken the care of weak souls, not a tyranny over those who are strong. He should fear the threat made by God through the prophet when he says, 'You took what you saw was fat, and you threw away what was weak' (Eze. 34:3, 4). Let him imitate the loving example of the good shepherd who left the ninety-nine sheep on the mountainside and went in search of the one sheep that had wandered off: he took such pity on its weakness that he deigned to place it on his own sacred shoulders and to carry it back to the flock in this way (Luke 15:4–5).

28

Those who refuse to amend despite frequent rebuke

If a brother has been frequently reprimanded for some fault but has not amended his ways even after being excommunicated, then he should undergo more severe punishment; in other words, he should be punished with beatings. But if he still does not correct his behaviour or if he perhaps tries arrogantly to defend his behaviour (which God forbid), then the abbot should follow the procedure of an experienced doctor. If he has applied the poultices and ointments of stern encouragement, if he has administered the medicine of the holy Scriptures, if finally he has carried out the cautery of excommunication or beatings, and if he then sees that his efforts are unsuccessful, he must also apply the more powerful remedy of his prayers and those of all the brothers on behalf of this brother, so that the Lord who can do all things might cure the one who is sick.

But if even these measures fail to cure him, then the abbot must use the knife of amputation: as the Apostle said, 'Banish the wrongdoer from among you' (1 Cor. 5:13), and similarly, 'If the unbeliever departs, let him depart' (1 Cor. 7:15), to prevent a single diseased sheep infecting the whole flock.

29

Readmission of brothers who leave the monastery

If a brother who leaves the monastery through his own fault wishes to return, he must first promise to make amends fully for the offence that caused him to leave. Then he may be received back – but at the lowest level, to put his humility to the test. If he leaves again, he should be received back up to three times, but he should be aware that after that he will be denied all possibility of return.

30

Correction of the young

Each age and level of understanding ought to have an appropriate measure of discipline. And so when an offence is committed by boys or young people or those who are unable to understand how severe a punishment excommunication is, they should either be punished by means of severe fasting or chastised with harsh beatings to cure them.

31

What kind of person the monastery's cellarer should be

As cellarer of the monastery one ought to choose from the community a man who is wise, mature and sensible. He must not be greedy, arrogant, a trouble-maker, or someone who causes offence to others or is inefficient or wasteful; instead he must be someone who fears God and will be like a father to the whole community. Let him be in charge of everything, but he must do nothing without the abbot's orders and must keep to his instructions. He must not upset the brothers. If a brother happens to make an unreasonable demand of him, he should not upset him by treating him with contempt but should refuse the inappropriate request in a reasonable and humble manner. He should keep watch over his own soul, always remembering the Apostle's saying that 'he who carries out his duties well will obtain a high standing for himself' (1 Tim. 3:13). He should take the greatest care of the sick, of children, guests and the poor, knowing for certain that he will have to give an account of all of these on the Day of Judgement. He must treat all the monastery's utensils and property as if they were sacred altar vessels. He must not think that he can neglect anything. He must not be greedy nor wasteful and extravagant with the monastery's property, but should do everything with moderation and in accordance with the abbot's orders.

Above all he must be humble and if he has nothing else to give, let him offer a kind word in reply, as it says in Scripture, 'A kind word is of more value than the best gift' (Sir. 18:17). He should be responsible for everything the abbot has assigned to him but should not presume to deal with things the abbot has forbidden. He should offer the brothers their portions of food promptly and without any self-importance, which might cause resentment, for he must bear in mind what the Lord says the person deserves 'who leads astray one of these little ones' (Matt. 18:6).

If the community is quite large, the cellarer should be given assistants, so that with their help he can calmly carry out the duties of his office. Necessary items should be requested and given at the proper times, so that no one is disturbed or distressed in the house of God.

32

The monastery's tools and property

The abbot should take care to put brothers whose behaviour and character he trusts in charge of the monastery's property; in other words, the tools, clothing and everything else. He should entrust to them each thing, as he thinks fit, to be looked after and collected back again. The abbot should keep a list of all the items, so that when the brothers take over from each other in the duties assigned them, he may know what he is handing out and what is being returned. If anyone treats the monastery property in a slovenly or careless manner, he should be reprimanded, and if he does not correct his behaviour, he must be subjected to the discipline of the rule.

33

The question of private ownership

It is vitally important to eradicate this bad practice from the monastery: no one should presume to give or receive anything without the abbot's permission, or to possess anything of his own – nothing whatever, not a book or writing tablet or pen or anything at all, for monks should not even count their own bodies and wills as their own. They must depend on the father of the monastery to provide everything they need. They are not allowed to have anything that the abbot has not given or permitted. As Scripture says, 'Let everything be held in common' (Acts 4:32), so no one should dare to claim private ownership of any possession. If anyone is found to be indulging in this wicked practice he should be rebuked once and a second time, but if he does not give it up, he must be punished.

34

The question of distribution according to need

We should act in accordance with Scripture when it says, 'It was divided among them according to the needs of each' (Acts 4:35), but by this we do not mean that there should be favouritism (which God forbid); instead, each person's weaknesses should be taken into consideration. If someone needs less, he should thank God and not be discontented, while someone who needs more should show humility because of his weakness and not become proud because he has been shown compassion. In this way the whole community will be at peace. Above all, there must be no word or sign of grumbling for any reason at all – this is a serious offence: if anyone is guilty of it, he should be subjected to strict discipline.

35

The weekly kitchen servers

The brothers should serve one another and no one should be excused from kitchen duty, unless he is sick or is busy with something particularly important, for by serving one another the brothers gain a greater reward and become more loving. But the weaker brothers should be given help, so that they do not find the task oppressive – in fact, all the brothers should have help, according to the size of the community and the local conditions. If the community is quite large, the cellarer should be excused from kitchen duty, and also those who, as we mentioned, are busy with important matters. The rest should serve one another in love. When one brother is about to finish his week's service, he should do the washing on a Saturday. He must wash the linen the brothers use to wipe their hands and feet. And everyone's feet should be washed by the one who is finishing his week's duty and the one who is starting it. The one who is finishing must give back to the cellarer the utensils of his office in a clean and undamaged state; the cellarer will then give them to the brother who is starting his week's duty – this will ensure that the cellarer can keep track of what he is handing out and what is returned.

An hour before the meal the weekly servers should each receive a drink and some bread in addition to the regular allowance, so that they can serve their brothers at the meal without grumbling or hardship; but on feast-days they must wait until after Mass. On Sundays, as soon as Lauds is finished, the ingoing and outgoing servers should kneel in front of everybody in the oratory and ask for their prayers. A server who is finishing his week's duty should recite this verse, Blessed are you, Lord

God, 'for you have helped me and consoled me' (Ps. 86:17), and when he has said this three times, he should receive a blessing. Then the brother who is starting his period of duty should say, 'God, come to my assistance; Lord, hasten to help me' (Ps. 70:1), and when he has said this three times, he should receive a blessing and start upon his duties.

36

Sick brothers

The care of the sick must take precedence over everything else, so that they may be served just like Christ, for Christ said, 'I was sick and you visited me' (Matt. 25:36) and 'What you did for one of these, insignificant though they be, you did for me' (Matt. 25:40). For their part the sick should consider that they are being served out of reverence for God and must not irritate the brothers who are serving them by making unreasonable demands. One must, however, put up with them patiently because greater rewards are derived from people like this. The abbot should therefore take the greatest care that no one is neglected.

A special room should be assigned to brothers who are sick, together with someone to attend to them who is God-fearing, loving and attentive. The sick should be allowed to take a bath whenever necessary, but those who are healthy, especially the younger brothers, should only be allowed a bath occasionally. Those who are very weak should be allowed to eat meat to regain their strength, but when they are better they should abstain from meat as usual. The abbot should take the greatest care that the cellarers and attendants do not neglect the sick, for he is responsible for all the failures of his disciples.

37

The elderly and children

Although people naturally show compassion towards old people and children, the authority of the rule should also provide for them. One should always bear in mind their weakness and, with regard to food, the rule should certainly not be applied very strictly to them. Rather, they should be treated with loving consideration and allowed to eat before the regular hours.

38

The weekly reader

The brothers' meals should always be accompanied by reading, not by a person at random who just picks up the book, but by someone who will read for the whole week, starting on a Sunday. After Mass and Communion, the one who is starting his period of duty should ask all the brothers to pray for him, so that God may preserve him from a spirit of pride, and then everyone in the oratory should repeat this verse after him three times, 'O Lord, open my lips, and my mouth will show forth your praise' (Ps. 51:15). Then he will receive a blessing and start reading. There must be complete silence and no whispering, so that only the reader's voice can be heard in the room. The brothers should supply each other with what they need while they are eating and drinking, so that no one needs to ask for anything. If, however, anything is required, it should be requested by some sign rather than by words. Unless a superior wants to give a few words of explanation, no one should venture to ask any questions about the reading or anything else, in case this encourages talking. The brother who is reading for the week should receive a little to eat and drink before he begins to read, because of Holy Communion,[1] and so that he does not find it too difficult to wait for his food. Afterwards he should take his meal with the kitchen workers and attendants of the week. Not all the brothers should take turns to read or sing – only those who are worth listening to.

39

The proper amount of food

We believe it is sufficient if at the daily meals, both at the sixth and ninth hour, every table has a choice of two cooked dishes to take account of different people's weaknesses: if someone is by chance unable to eat one of them, he can be restored by the other. And so two cooked dishes should be enough for all the brothers, and if there is any fruit or young vegetables, these may be added as a third dish. One pound of bread should be enough for the day, whether there is a single meal or both dinner and supper. If the brothers are going to have supper, the cellarer should keep a third part of the pound of bread to give them at supper. But if their workload happens to have been heavier, the abbot can decide, if he thinks it right, to use his authority to increase this allowance. Over-indulgence must be avoided above all things to prevent any monk suffering from indigestion, for there is nothing so inappropriate for a Christian as over-indulgence, as our Lord says, 'Make sure that your hearts are not weighed down by over-indulgence' (Luke 21:34). The younger children should not be given the same sized portions: they should receive less than their elders and frugality should be the rule in all circumstances. Everyone, apart from those who are very weak, should abstain completely from eating the meat of four-footed animals.

40

The proper amount of drink

'Each person has his own gift from God – one person has one kind of gift and the next person has a different one' (1 Cor. 7:7). It is therefore with some uneasiness that we make rules as to how much others should eat or drink; but bearing in mind the needs of the weaker brothers, we think that half a bottle of wine a day is enough for each person. But those to whom God grants the ability to abstain should know that they will have their own reward. It is up to the superior to decide whether local conditions, the work or summer heat mean that more is required, but he must always make sure that no one over-indulges or gets drunk. We read that wine is not a suitable drink[1] for monks, but since monks nowadays cannot be persuaded of this, let us at least agree to drink sparingly and not to excess, because wine causes even sensible people to behave foolishly. When local conditions mean that it is impossible even to have this amount but only much less or none at all, then those who live there should bless God and not grumble: above all, we urge them that there should be no grumbling.

41

Meal times

From the holy feast of Easter to Pentecost, the brothers should have dinner at the sixth hour and a late supper. From Pentecost throughout the summer, if the monks have no work to do in the fields or if the summer heat is oppressive, they should fast on Wednesdays and Fridays until the ninth hour, while on the other days they should dine at the sixth hour. The abbot may decide that eating at the sixth hour every day should be the practice, if there is work to do in the fields or if the summer heat is extreme. He must arrange and manage everything in such a way that souls may be saved and that the brothers do what they have to do without having cause to grumble. From 13 September[1] until the beginning of Lent, the meal should always take place at the ninth hour. In Lent until Easter the meal should be in the evening. However, Vespers should be timed in such a way that the brothers do not need lamplight while they are eating, but should finish everything while it is still daylight. At all times of the year, either supper or the time of the main meal should be scheduled so that everything can be done in daylight.

42

Silence after Compline

Monks should be silent at all times but especially at night. This should always be the rule, whether it is a fast day or not. If it is not a fast day, as soon as they have risen from supper they should all sit together, and one of them should read the *Conferences* or the *Lives of the Fathers*[1] or something else that will benefit the listeners, but not the Heptateuch or the books of Kings[2] because it will not be useful for impressionable minds to hear those parts of Scripture at that time of day: these parts should be read at other times. If it is a fast day, when Vespers is finished they should proceed after a short interval with the reading of the *Conferences*, as we mentioned. Four or five pages (or as many as time permits) should be read, and during this period everyone should have had time to gather, even if they happen to be busy with some task assigned to them.

When all have gathered, let them say Compline. When they leave after Compline, no one is allowed to say anything more. If anyone is found to be breaking this rule of silence, he will be severely punished unless it was necessary to speak because of the arrival of visitors or if the abbot gave someone an order. But even in this case it should be done with the utmost seriousness and restraint.

43

Latecomers to the work of God or to meals

As soon as the brothers hear the signal for the divine office, they should all stop what they are doing and hurry as fast as possible but in a dignified manner: there must be no fooling around. The work of God must take precedence over everything else. But if anyone arrives during the night office after the Gloria of Psalm 95 (which should be said very slowly and deliberately to allow everyone to arrive in time), he should not stand in his usual place in the choir but must stand right at the end or in a place apart, designated by the abbot for those who fail to do as they should. He must stand in full view of the abbot and everyone else until the work of God is finished and he can do penance in public. Our decision to make him stand at the end or apart was taken so that if he is in full view of everyone, he may be motivated by a sense of shame to correct his ways. If the culprits were to remain outside the oratory, some of them might move off and go to bed or at least sit down outside or spend their time chattering, thereby giving the devil an opportunity. They should go inside, so they do not miss the whole thing and may correct their ways for the future.

During the daytime services the same rule applies to someone who does not arrive at the work of God until after the verse and the Gloria of the first psalm following the verse: he must stand right at the end, and he should not venture to join the choir in singing until he has made amends, unless the abbot has pardoned him and given him permission. Even in this case the one who is guilty must do penance afterwards.

When someone fails to come to the table before the blessing, thereby preventing everyone from saying the verse and prayers together and going to table at the same time, if his failure to arrive is the result of carelessness or his own fault, he should be reprimanded for this once or even twice, but if he still fails to correct his ways, he should not be allowed to partake of the shared meal, but must eat apart from everyone else without any company and be deprived of his allowance of wine until he has made amends and corrected his ways. Anyone who was not present at the verse said after the meal should be treated in the same way. Let no one presume to take any food or drink before or after the appointed hour. However, if someone is offered something by his superior and refuses it, then when he wants what he earlier refused or anything else, he should receive nothing at all until he has made suitable amends.

44

How the excommunicated should make amends

If a brother is excommunicated from the oratory and from meals for a serious offence, he should lie prostrate in silence in front of the oratory doors during the divine service, lying face down at the feet of all the brothers as they come out of the oratory. He should continue to do this until the abbot judges that he has made sufficient amends. When he is told by the abbot to come in to the oratory, he should throw himself at the abbot's feet and then at the feet of everyone else, so that they may pray for him. And then, if the abbot so orders, he should be received into the choir, in the place the abbot assigns him. Even so he should not venture to lead a psalm or do the reading or anything else in the oratory unless the abbot tells him to. At each of the services, at the end of the work of God, he should prostrate himself on the ground in his place, and in this way he should make amends until the abbot gives the order for him to stop. Those who have committed minor offences and are excommunicated only from the meal should make amends in the oratory until the abbot tells them to stop. They should continue until he gives a blessing and says, 'That is enough.'

45

Mistakes in the oratory

If anyone makes a mistake in reciting a psalm, responsory, antiphon or reading and does not make reparation humbly in front of everyone, he should be punished more severely for refusing to correct by humility the mistake he made through carelessness. But if a child makes a mistake of this kind he should be beaten.

46

Offences committed elsewhere

If anyone in the course of whatever work he might be doing, whether in the kitchen, the cellar, in serving, in the bakehouse, or in the garden or in any other place, either breaks something or loses it[1] or does something else wrong, and if he does not immediately come forward before the abbot and community, admit his error and do penance for it of his own accord, and if his error is only discovered by someone else, then he must be punished more severely. If the cause of the sin is hidden in his soul, then he should tell only the abbot or a spiritual father, for they know how to heal their own wounds and those of others without revealing them and making them public.

47

Announcing the time for the work of God

It is the abbot's duty to announce the hour of the work of God during the day and at night. He should either announce it himself or assign this task to a brother who will ensure that everything is done at the right time. Those who have been ordered to do so should lead the psalms and antiphons in turn after the abbot. No one should venture to sing or read unless he can fulfil this duty in such a way as to benefit those who are listening. It should be done with humility, seriousness and reverence by the one whom the abbot has asked to do it.

48

Daily manual labour

Idleness is the enemy of the soul and so the brothers ought to engage in manual labour at set times, and at other times in biblical study.[1] We believe that the times for both should be arranged as follows. From Easter until 1 October the brothers should go out in the morning and work from the first until about the fourth hour, as necessary. From the fourth hour until about the sixth hour, they should spend the time reading. After the sixth hour, when they leave the table they must rest on their beds in complete silence, or if anyone wants to read by himself, he must do so in a way that does not disturb anyone else. The service of None should be said early, half-way through the eighth hour, and then the brothers should work at what needs to be done until Vespers. If local conditions or poverty require them to gather in the harvest themselves, they should not be despondent, because it is when they live by the work of their hands, like our fathers and the apostles, that they are truly monks. But everything should be done in moderation to allow for the weaker brothers.

From 1 October until the beginning of Lent, they should spend the time reading until the end of the second hour. At that point Terce should be said, and all the brothers should then work until None at the tasks assigned to them. When the first signal has been given for the ninth hour, they should all stop what they are doing and wait in readiness for the second signal. After the meal they should devote themselves to reading or to the psalms.

During Lent they should spend the morning reading until the end of the third hour, and then they should work on the tasks assigned them until the end of the tenth hour. During Lent they should all be given a book from the library which they should read from cover to cover. These books should be handed out at the beginning of Lent. It is very important that one or two of the older monks be appointed to go round the monastery during the period when the brothers are reading, to check that no one is being lazy and wasting his time doing nothing or chatting rather than concentrating on his reading, for not only does he derive no benefit from this himself but he also distracts others. If they come across such a person (which God forbid), he should be reprimanded once and even a second time, but if he does not correct his ways he should be subjected to the punishment of the rule, as a warning to the others. The brothers should not be in each other's company at inappropriate times.

On Sundays they should all spend time reading, apart from those who have been assigned various tasks. But if anyone is so lacking in concentration and so lazy that he refuses or is unable to study or read, he should be given a task to prevent him being idle. Brothers who are weak or delicate should be given a task or craft that prevents them being idle but does not cause them to feel oppressed by the difficulty of the task or to try to avoid it. The abbot should have consideration for their weakness.

49

Observance of Lent

The life of a monk ought at all times to be Lenten in its observances but because few have the strength for this, we urge that in Lent they should maintain a life of complete purity to make up, during these holy days, for all the careless practices throughout the rest of the year. We can achieve this if we refrain from all sin and put all our effort into prayer accompanied by tears, into reading, compunction of heart and abstinence. And so during these days let us increase the amount of our service, by going further in the way of special prayers and abstinence from food and drink, so that each person, of his own free will, offers to God something more than usual, with the joy of the Holy Spirit. In other words he must cut down on food, drink, sleep, talkativeness, joking, and should look forward to holy Easter with the joy of spiritual longing. Each brother must tell the abbot what he is offering and ask for the abbot's blessing and consent, because whatever is done without the father's permission might be attributed to unwarranted pride and a desire for self-glorification rather than to any reward. And so everything ought to be done with the abbot's approval.

50

Brothers working or travelling far from the oratory

If any brothers are working far away and cannot get to the oratory at the right time and if the abbot recognizes that this is the case, then they should perform the work of God in their place of work, kneeling down in reverence before God. Similarly those who have been sent on a journey should not neglect the appointed hours but should say the liturgy to themselves if possible and not neglect to pay the due measure of service.

51

Brothers on a short journey

A brother who is sent out on some errand and is expected to return to the monastery the same day should not eat while away, even if someone invites him to do so, unless it happens that his abbot has told him to. If he does not obey, he should be excommunicated.

52

The monastery oratory

The oratory should be just what its name implies and nothing else should be done or stored there. When the work of God is finished, everyone should leave the oratory in complete silence, showing reverence for God, so that any brother who perhaps wishes to pray by himself is not hindered by someone else's lack of restraint. But if someone wishes to pray alone at any other time, he should just go in and pray, not in a loud voice but with tears and spiritual concentration. Anyone who does not pray in this manner should not be allowed to remain in the oratory when the work of God is finished, to prevent him being a nuisance to anyone else, as we have said.

53

The reception of guests

All guests who arrive should be received as if they were Christ, for he will say, 'I was a stranger and you took me in' (Matt. 25:35). Each person should be treated with respect, particularly pilgrims and those 'who share the faith' (Gal. 6:10). So when a guest arrives, the superior or some of the brothers should go to meet him and treat him with all courtesy and love. First of all they should pray together so as to be united in peace. The kiss of peace should not be offered until the prayers have been said, to prevent the devil deluding them. In greeting those who are arriving or departing, the greatest humility should be shown: the brothers should bow the head or prostrate the whole body, and in this way Christ should be worshipped in guests, for it is he who is welcomed in their person.

When the guests have been welcomed, they should be taken to prayer and then the superior (or someone to whom he delegates this task) should sit with them. The law of God should be read to the guest for his edification, and after this all kindness should be shown to him. The superior can break his fast for the sake of his guest, unless it happens to be an important fast day which cannot be violated. The brothers, however, should observe the customary fasts. The abbot should give the guests water for their hands, and the abbot as well as the whole community should wash all the guests' feet; after washing them, they should say this verse, 'O God, we have received your mercy in the midst of your temple' (Ps. 48:9).

Special care and attention should be shown in the reception of the poor and of pilgrims because in such people Christ is more truly welcomed. When it comes to rich people we are more likely to show them respect because we are in awe of them.

There should be a separate kitchen for the abbot and guests, so that if guests (of which a monastery will never have a shortage) turn up at odd times, they will not disturb the brothers. Two brothers who are suitably competent should be deputed to work in this kitchen for a year at a time, and they should be given assistance when they need it, so that they can do their work without grumbling. When they have less work to do, they should go out and do whatever task has been assigned them. In fact assistance should be given not only to them when they need it, but to all those who have duties to perform in the monastery, and when they have spare time, they too should obediently do anything they are told to do.

A brother whose heart is filled with the fear of God should be assigned to look after the guest-house where there should be enough beds ready. The house of God should be looked after by sensible people in a sensible way. No one should associate with guests or converse with them unless he is told to do so. But if a brother meets or sees a visitor, he should greet him with humility, as we said, and ask for a blessing as he passes, explaining that he is not permitted to converse with a guest.

54

Letters or gifts for monks

A monk should on no account be allowed to receive letters, gifts, or any little tokens from his parents or from anyone else, or to send them in return without the abbot's permission. If he is sent something by his parents, he must not accept it before he has shown it to the abbot. If permission is given for it to be accepted, it is up to the abbot to decide whom to give it to; the brother to whom it was sent should not be upset or he might 'give an opportunity to the devil' (Eph. 4:27). Anyone who presumes to do otherwise must submit to the discipline of the rule.

55

The brothers' clothing and footwear

The clothing given to the brothers should be appropriate for the conditions of the place where they live and the local climate, because they will need to wear more in cold areas and less in warm places. It is up to the abbot to take this into consideration. We believe that normally it will be enough for each of the monks to have a tunic and a cowl (a woollen hood in winter, and a thin or old one in the summer) and a scapular for work; on their feet they should wear shoes and socks. The monks should not complain about the colour or thickness of all these items but be content with what is to be found locally and what can be bought cheaply. With regard to the size, the abbot should take care that the clothes are not too short but are the right size for the person wearing them. When the brothers receive new ones they should always hand in the old ones at once, so that they can be put away in the clothes room for the poor. It is enough for each monk to have two tunics and two cowls, so that he has a change for night wear and to allow for washing. Anything more is superfluous and ought to be removed. They should hand in their shoes and anything else that is old when they receive new ones. Those who are sent on a journey should receive underpants from the clothes room, which they should wash and hand back on their return. The tunics and cowls they receive from the clothes room when they go off on their journey should be slightly better than the ones they usually wear; these, too, they must hand back on their return.

As for bedding, it is enough for them to have a mat, together with a blanket, a cover and a pillow. The abbot should inspect the beds frequently to check for personal property, and if anything is found which the brother did not receive from the abbot, he must be punished severely. So as to eradicate this vice utterly, the abbot should hand out everything that is needed; in other words, cowls, tunics, shoes, socks, belt, knife, pen, needle, handkerchief and writing tablets: then no one can pretend that they have need of something. The abbot, however, should always remember the passage from the Acts of the Apostles where it says that 'things were given to each person according to his needs' (Acts 4:35). And so the abbot should take into account the weakness of those who are in need, rather than the ill-will of the envious. In all his decisions he must bear in mind God's retribution.

56

The abbot's table

The abbot should always eat with the guests and pilgrims, but when there are no guests he has the right to invite any of the brothers he wishes to. However, one or two of the older brothers should always be left with the others to maintain discipline.

57

The monastery craftsmen

If there are any craftsmen in the monastery, let them practise their crafts with complete humility, as long as the abbot gives his permission. But if one of them becomes arrogant because he is skilled at his craft, believing that he is benefiting the monastery, he should be removed from that craft and not allowed to resume it until he has shown humility and the abbot tells him he can. If any of the craftsmen's work is to be sold, those who are responsible for arranging the transaction should take care not to act dishonestly. They should always remember the example of Ananias and Saphira,[1] so that they (or anyone else who commits some fraud with monastery property) do not suffer the same death in their souls as these two suffered in their body. As for the price, the sin of avarice must not be allowed to creep in: instead, things should always be sold a little more cheaply than they can be sold by people outside the monastery, so that in all things God may be glorified.

58

Regulations regarding the admission of brothers

Newcomers to the monastic life should not be granted easy entry, but as the Apostle says, 'Test the spirits to see whether they are from God' (1 John 4:1). If the newcomer persists in knocking and seems to endure patiently the harsh treatment and the difficulty of entry, and if he continues to make his petition, then he should be allowed in and permitted to stay for a few days in the guest-house. After this he should stay in the novices' centre, where they study and eat and sleep. An older brother who is skilled at gaining souls should be assigned to watch over them with the greatest care. He must make sure that the novice is really seeking God and find out whether he is keen to perform the work of God, to be obedient and to be treated in a humbling manner. The novice should be told about all the difficult and harsh things he will experience along the road to God.

If he promises to persevere with his intention, after two months this rule should be read through to him, and he should be told, 'This is the law under which you wish to serve; if you are able to keep it, enter, but if you cannot, you are free to go.' If he still persists, then he should be taken into the novices' centre we mentioned and his patience tested again in every way. After six months the rule should be read to him so that he knows what he is letting himself in for. If he still stands firm, after four months the same rule should be read to him yet again. If, after careful consideration, he promises to observe all the rules and to obey all the commands given to him, then he should be received into the community, in full awareness of the fact that the law of the rule lays down that from that day on he is not allowed to leave the monastery or to withdraw his neck from the yoke of the rule, which he had been allowed to accept or reject during the extended period of reflection.

The one who is to be received should take a vow in the oratory in front of everyone: he must promise stability, conversion of his way of life and obedience before God and his saints, so that if he ever does otherwise, he will be clear that he will be condemned by the one whom he scorns. Regarding this promise he should make a petition in the name of the saints whose relics are in that monastery and of the abbot who is present. He should write this petition in his own hand or, if he is illiterate, he must ask someone else to do it for him, and then the novice should put his mark to it and place it on the altar with his own hand. On placing it there, the novice should immediately start to say this verse, 'Receive me, O Lord, according to your words, and I will live; do not disappoint me in my hope' (Ps. 119:116). The whole community should repeat this verse three times, adding 'Glory be to the Father'. Then the novice brother must prostrate himself at the feet of each brother, so that they can pray for him, and from this day on he should be reckoned to be part of the community.

If he possesses any property, he should first distribute it to the poor or make a formal donation granting it to the monastery, keeping absolutely nothing for himself, for he should be aware that from that day on he will not even have jurisdiction over his own body. That is why he will be stripped of his own clothes in the oratory and dressed in the clothes of the monastery. The clothes he takes off will be placed for safe-keeping in the clothes room, so that if at some point he listens to the devil's persuasions and leaves the monastery (which God forbid), then he will have to take off the monastic clothes before he is expelled. However, the petition the abbot took from the altar will not be returned to him but will be kept in the monastery.

59

The offering of their sons by nobles or by the poor

Should it happen that a nobleman offers his son to God in the monastery and if the boy is still very young, his parents should make the petition we mentioned above. When they make the offering, they should wrap the petition and the boy's hand in the altar cloth and offer him in this way. As to his property, let them promise in this same petition under oath that they will never themselves or through an intermediary or by any other means give him anything or provide him with an opportunity to possess anything. If they are unwilling to do this and they wish to offer something as alms to the monastery so as to gain a reward, they should make a donation from what they want to give to the monastery, retaining for themselves, should they so wish, the use and revenue during their lifetime. In this way they will prevent the boy having any expectations whatsoever which might deceive and ruin him (which God forbid), as experience has taught us. Poor people should do the same, but those who possess nothing at all should simply make a petition and offer their son in the presence of witnesses when the offering is made.

60

The admission of priests to the monastery

If anyone who has been ordained a priest asks to be received into the monastery, he should not be granted permission too readily, but if he persists in his request, he needs to be aware that he will have to observe the full discipline of the rule and that he will be allowed no relaxation of the rules, for as it says in Scripture, 'My friend, what have you come for?' (Matt. 26:50). He will, however, be allowed to take his place next to the abbot and to give blessings and celebrate mass, if the abbot tells him to. Otherwise he should not take it upon himself to do anything, knowing that he is subject to the discipline of the rule and that he should instead be giving an example of humility to the others. If it happens that there is the question of an appointment or other business in the monastery, he must take his place according to the date of his entry into the monastery rather than the position granted to him out of respect for him as a priest. If any clerics wish to join the monastery out of a similar desire, they should be assigned a middle rank, but they are to be admitted only if they promise to observe the rule and maintain their commitment to stability.

61

The reception of visiting monks

If a monk who arrives on a visit from distant regions wishes to live in the monastery as a guest and is happy to accept the customs of the place as he finds them and does not disturb the monastery with his excessive demands but is simply content with what he finds, then he should be allowed to stay for as long as he wishes. If with good reason and in a spirit of loving humility, he criticizes or points out any defect, the abbot should consider the matter fairly in case the Lord has perhaps sent the person for this purpose. If later on he wishes to confirm his commitment to stay in one place, this wish should not be rejected, especially as the quality of his life will have been discerned during the period when he was a guest.

But if he is found to be demanding or problematic during his time as a guest, then not only should he not join the monastic community but he should be asked politely to leave, so that the others are not corrupted by his unacceptable behaviour. If he does not deserve to be dismissed, then he should be accepted as a member of the community if he asks to join, and he should in fact be persuaded to remain, so that the others can learn from his example: after all, wherever we are we serve the same Lord and fight for the same King. If the abbot considers him worthy, he may accord him a slightly higher position. In fact the abbot can give monks as well as those who have been ordained as priests or clergy a higher position than they had on entry, if he considers them worthy. But the abbot must be careful not to allow a monk from another known monastery to come and live there unless he has his abbot's permission or a letter of recommendation, for as it says in Scripture, 'Do not do to someone else what you do not want done to you' (Tob. 4:15).

62

Priests of the monastery

If an abbot wishes to have a priest or deacon ordained, he should choose one of the brothers whom he considers worthy to perform the duties of the priesthood. When this brother has been ordained, he must take care to avoid self-satisfaction or pride and must not presume to do anything apart from what the abbot has told him to do, knowing well that he must be all the more subject to the discipline of the rule. The fact that he is a priest must not cause him to forget the obedience and discipline demanded by the rule; in fact he must try to make even more progress towards God.

He should always keep the place he was given on entry to the monastery, except in his duties at the altar and unless the community has voted and the abbot has agreed that he should be promoted on account of the excellence of his life. However, he should be aware that he must observe the rules set for the deans and priors; if he presumes to act otherwise, he will not be regarded as a priest but a rebel, and if after repeated warnings he does not correct his behaviour, the bishop should also be brought in as a witness. If he still does not improve and still has glaring faults, he must be expelled from the monastery, should his obstinacy be such that he refuses to submit and obey the rule.

63

Rank within the community

In the monastery the brothers should keep the rank they were assigned at the time of their entry to the monastic life, according to the merits of their life or as the abbot decides. The abbot must not disturb the flock entrusted to him or make any unjust arrangements as if he had arbitrary power, but always bear in mind that he will have to give an account to God of all his decisions and actions. And so when the brothers come forward for the kiss of peace, for communion, or to intone the psalm or when they are standing in the choir, they should keep to the order the abbot has decided on or which the brothers themselves keep to. In no circumstances whatsoever should age make a difference to the order or prejudice it: after all, Samuel and Daniel[1] judged their elders, even though they were only boys. Apart from those whom, as we mentioned, the abbot has decided, after careful consideration, to promote or demote for a particular reason, all the rest should keep the rank assigned to them at their entry into the monastic life, so that for example someone who entered the monastery at the second hour of the day, should recognize that he is junior to someone who arrived at the first hour, regardless of his age and social status. The boys, however, are to be subject at all times to the discipline of everyone.

The younger ones must respect their seniors and the older ones must love the younger ones. In addressing one another no one must call someone just by his name: the older ones must call the younger ones 'brother' and the younger ones should call their elders 'nonnus',[2] which means 'reverend father'. The abbot, because he is Christ's representative, should be called 'lord' and 'abbot', not because of his high position but out of reverence and love for Christ. He must bear this in mind and show himself worthy of such honour.

Whenever the brothers meet each other, the younger one should ask the older one for a blessing. If an older brother passes by, the younger one should stand up and give him his seat and the younger one should not presume to sit down unless the older one tells him to. In this way Scripture will be fulfilled when it says, 'Be eager to give precedence to each other' (Rom. 12:10). Small boys and adolescents must strictly maintain their proper order in the oratory and at table. Outside or anywhere else they must be supervised and controlled, until they reach the age of discretion.

64

Election of the abbot

In the appointment of an abbot, the guiding principle should always be that the person appointed should be the one chosen unanimously by the whole congregation in the fear of God, or even by a minority, however small, of the community if they will make the more sensible decision. The one to be appointed should be chosen for his virtuous way of life and the wisdom of his teaching, even if he is the lowest in rank in the community. But if the whole community agrees to choose someone who condones their vices (which God forbid) and those vices come to the attention of the bishop to whose diocese that place belongs, or of the neighbouring abbots and Christians, they must prevent this conspiracy of the wicked taking control, and must appoint someone suitable to be in charge of the house of God, knowing that they will be well rewarded for this, if they do it with pure intentions and with enthusiasm for God. Conversely, they will be guilty if they fail to act.

Once the abbot has been appointed, he must always consider the burden he has undertaken and to whom he will have to 'give an account of his stewardship' (Luke 16:2). He must be aware that it is his duty to benefit others rather than to control them. It is his duty to be learned in the divine law so that he may be knowledgeable and have a store from which he can 'take out new things and old' (Matt. 13:52); he must also be pure, sensible and merciful. He must always 'put mercy before judgement' (James 2:13), so that he himself may also be shown mercy. He must hate wrongdoing and love the brothers. When punishing he must act sensibly and not be excessive, in case he should damage the pot while trying to scrub away the dirt. He must always distrust his own fragility and remember not to 'crush the bruised reed' (Isa. 42:3). By this we do not mean that he should allow wrongdoings to grow rampant but should eradicate them sensibly and with love, in accordance with what seems beneficial to each, as we have mentioned. He should strive to be loved rather than feared. He must not be inconsistent or anxious, not extreme in his behaviour or obstinate, not jealous or excessively suspicious, for then he will never rest. He must act with foresight and consideration whenever he gives an order. Whether the task he orders concerns God or the world, he should be discreet and restrained, remembering the discretion of holy Jacob who said, 'If I drive my flocks too hard, they will all die on a single day' (Gen. 33:13). Taking these and other examples of discretion, the mother of all virtues, let him be moderate in all things, so that the stronger brothers still have something to work towards and the weaker ones will not be put off. In particular, he should observe this rule in all things. Then his wise management will mean that he will hear from the Lord what the good servant heard who distributed wheat to his fellow servants at the right time: 'Truly, I say to you, he has put him in charge of all his possessions' (Matt. 24:47).

65

The prior of the monastery

It frequently happens that the appointment of a prior gives rise to serious scandals in the monasteries, for there are some who are puffed up with a wicked spirit of pride and consider themselves on a par with the abbots, arrogating to themselves tyrannical power. In this way they feed scandal and cause dissension in the community, especially in monasteries where the prior is appointed by the same bishop and abbots as the abbot himself. It is easy to see how absurd this is for it means that he is given reason to be proud from the moment of his appointment, since he will think to himself, 'I have been appointed by the same people as the abbot', and that he is therefore not subject to the abbot's power. This will cause envy, quarrels, back-biting, rivalry, dissension and breaches of the rule, and whenever the abbot and prior disagree their souls must be in danger as a result of their dissension. The monks for whom they are responsible will also be heading towards damnation when they try to take sides. Responsibility for this dangerous situation lies chiefly with those who set up this confusing practice.

We therefore think it a good idea to preserve peace and love by putting the abbot in charge of appointments in his monastery. If possible all practical matters within the monastery should be dealt with by the deans, as mentioned earlier, under the supervision of the abbot, so that if the business is entrusted to several, no individual will have reason to become proud. But if circumstances demand or the community makes a reasonable and humble request and the abbot considers it the right course, then the abbot, with the advice of the God-fearing brothers, should choose someone and appoint him as his prior.

However, this prior should respectfully do whatever his abbot tells him to do and not do anything contrary to the abbot's wishes or his arrangements, for the higher the position conferred on him, the more careful he ought to be to observe the precepts of the rule.

If the prior is found to have serious faults or is seduced by conceit into being proud or is proved to be treating this holy rule with contempt, he should be admonished verbally as many as four times, but if he does not mend his ways, then he should be punished according to the discipline of the rule. If he still does not correct his behaviour, then he must be dismissed from the office of prior and replaced by someone more suitable. But if he fails to be quiet and obedient within the community after this, then he must be expelled even from the monastery. However, the abbot should bear in mind that he must give to God an account of all his judgements: this should prevent his soul becoming inflamed by envy or rivalry.

66

The porter of the monastery

A wise old man should be placed at the monastery gate, who will know how to take a message and give a reply and whose age means that he will not be tempted to wander about. This porter should have a room next to the gate so that anyone who arrives will always find someone there to deal with enquiries. As soon as someone knocks or a poor man calls him, he should reply, 'Thanks be to God' or 'Your blessing, please'. His response should be given promptly and with great gentleness, inspired by fear of God and with the warmth of love. If this porter needs help, one of the younger brothers should provide assistance.

If possible, the monastery should be arranged in such a way that everything necessary – in other words, water, the mill, the garden and the various crafts practised – should be inside the monastery, so that the monks do not need to go wandering outside for that is not at all good for their souls.

We would like this rule to be read aloud frequently in the community, so that no brother can plead ignorance as an excuse.

67

Brothers sent on a journey

Brothers who are to be sent on a journey should commend themselves to the prayers of the abbot and all the brothers. All those who are absent should be remembered in the last prayer of the work of God. On the same day the brothers return from their journey, they should lie prostrate on the floor of the oratory throughout all the canonical hours of the work of God. They must ask everyone to pray for them on account of any faults they may happen to have committed on their journey – if perhaps they witnessed something bad or heard something bad as the result of idle talk. No one should presume to tell anyone else what he saw or heard outside the monastery, for this can cause great harm. If someone does venture to do so, he should submit to the punishment of the rule. The same goes for anyone who dares to leave the enclosure of the monastery to go anywhere or to do anything however trivial without being instructed to do so by the abbot.

68

The assignment of impossible tasks to a brother

If a brother happens to be given difficult or impossible things to do, he should accept the command in complete humility and obedience, but if he realizes that the burden of the task definitely exceeds the limits of his strength, he should choose the right moment to explain patiently to the person in charge why it is impossible. However, he must not do it in an attitude of arrogance, obstinacy or rebelliousness. But if despite his explanation the superior persists in giving the same command, the junior should consider that it is for his own benefit, and should obey out of love, trusting in God's support.

69

*No one is to defend someone else in the
monastery*

Within the monastery measures should be taken to prevent
there being an opportunity for one monk to defend another or
to try to protect him, even if they are related. The monks must
in no way venture to do this because it can lead to serious
scandal. If anyone breaks this rule, he should be severely
punished.

70

No one is to strike someone else without due cause

Every occasion for over-confidence is to be avoided in the monastery, so we insist that no one is allowed to excommunicate or beat any of the brothers unless he has been given permission by the abbot. 'Those who offend must be reprimanded in front of everyone so that the others will have fear instilled in them' (1 Tim. 5:20). But boys up to the age of fifteen should be watched over and carefully disciplined by everyone, but always with moderation and in a sensible manner. Anyone who excommunicates or beats the older ones without the abbot's instruction, or who gets excessively angry with the younger ones, should submit to the punishment of the rule, for it says in Scripture, 'Do not do to someone else what you do not want done to you' (Tob. 4:15).

71

Mutual obedience

The virtue of obedience is not only to be practised by all towards the abbot but the brothers must also obey each other, aware that it is by walking along the path of obedience that they will reach God. Above all else they must respect the commands of the abbot or of those appointed by the abbot and must not allow unofficial orders to take precedence over them; for the rest, let all the juniors obey their seniors, showing them love and concern. But if someone is found to be quarrelsome, he must be punished. If one of the brothers, for the slightest reason, is punished in some way by the abbot or one of his superiors, or if he perceives that one of them is angry with him or the slightest bit displeased, he should immediately prostrate himself on the ground at his feet and lie there doing penance until a blessing is given which will heal the upset. If he disdains to do this, he must submit to corporal punishment or, if he is stubborn, he must be expelled from the monastery.

72

Beneficial fervour in a monk

Just as there is a reprehensible kind of fervour driven by bitterness which separates us from God and leads to hell, so there is a beneficial fervour which separates us from sin and leads to God and eternal life. This is the kind of zeal that the monks should practise with loving eagerness, striving to be the first to show each other respect. They must bear with great patience one another's weaknesses of body and character and compete with each other in being obedient. No one should pursue what he thinks will benefit himself but rather what benefits someone else; the brothers must demonstrate brotherly love in a virtuous manner; they must fear God and love their abbot with a sincere and humble love; and they must put Christ above all else so that he may lead us all alike to eternal life.

73

This rule is only a start on the path to justice

We have written this rule so that by living in accordance with it in monasteries we may demonstrate that we are to some extent living virtuously and have made a start on the religious life. But for someone who is in a hurry to attain perfection in this way of life, there are the teachings of the holy fathers: by observing these a man will be led to the heights of perfection. For is not every page and every word of divine authority in the Old and New Testaments a most reliable guide to human life? Do not all the books of the holy catholic fathers resonate with a desire to show us the direct route to our creator? What are the *Conferences*, the *Institutes* and the *Lives of the Fathers* as well as the *Rule* of our holy father Basil,[1] if not the tools of virtue for monks who wish to lead a virtuous and obedient life? But we are lazy and live reprehensible and careless lives, and we ought to be ashamed of ourselves. Whoever you are then, who are hurrying towards the heavenly country, observe this little rule for beginners which I have written with Christ's help, and then with God's protection you will at last reach the greater heights of wisdom and virtue I mentioned earlier in this work.

Appendix
Daily Services (Liturgy of the Hours) in Benedict's Monasteries

The table of services provides a guide as to the contents of each of the eight daily services and is derived from the brief, but often quite specific, information Benedict gives in Chapters 8–18 of his *Rule*. The content of each service might differ slightly depending on the day of the week and the time of year.

Night office (weekdays)
Chapters 9–10

(Begins at 8th hour of night)
Comprises:
verse of Scripture repeated
  3 times
Ps. 3 with Gloria
Ps. 95 with antiphon
Hymn
6 psalms with antiphons
verse and blessing
3 readings with 3 responsories
6 psalms with Alleluia
Reading from St Paul's Epistles
verse of Scripture
Kyrie Eleison

Night Office (Sundays)
Chapter 11

(Begins before 8th hour of night)
Comprises:
verse of Scripture repeated
  3 times
Ps. 3 with Gloria
Ps. 95 with antiphon
Hymn
6 psalms with antiphons
4 readings with responsories
6 psalms with antiphons
verse of Scripture
4 readings with responsories
3 canticles from prophets with
  Alleluia
verse and blessing
4 readings from New Testament
  with responsories
Te Deum laudamus
Reading from the Gospels
Te decet laus
Blessing

Lauds (weekdays)	*Lauds* (Sundays)
Chapter 13	Chapter 12

(Begins at dawn)	(Begins at dawn)
Comprises:	Comprises:
Ps 67 (without antiphon)	Ps. 67 with antiphon
Ps 51 with antiphon	Ps. 51 with Alleluia
2 psalms	Ps. 118 and Ps. 63
Canticle from Deuteronomy or prophets	*Benedicite*
	Psalms 148–150
Psalms 148–150	Reading from Revelation with responsory
Reading from St Paul's Epistles with responsory	Hymn
Hymn	verse
verse	Canticle from the Gospels
Canticle from the Gospels	*Kyrie Eleison*
Kyrie Eleison	Lord's Prayer
Lord's Prayer	

Prime, Terce, Sext, None
Chapter 17

(At about 6 a.m., 9 a.m., midday and 3 p.m.)
Comprise:
Verse of Scripture
Hymn
3 psalms, each with Gloria
Reading
Verse
Kyrie Eleison
Prayers

Vespers
Chapter 17

(At about 6 p.m.)
Comprises:
4 psalms with antiphons
Reading and responsory
Hymn
Verse
Canticle from the Gospels
Kyrie Eleison
Lord's Prayer

Compline
Chapter 17

(Before bedtime)
Comprises:
3 psalms (without antiphons)
Hymn
Reading
Verse
Kyrie Eleison
Blessing

Notes

For full bibliographical citations, see Further Reading.

ABBREVIATIONS

ECL	*Early Christian Lives*
PL	*Patrologia Latina*, ed. J. P. Migne (Paris, 1844–55), 221 volumes, containing editions of Christian ecclesiastical writings in Latin to 1216
RB	*The Rule of Benedict*
RB 1980	*RB 1980: The Rule of Saint Benedict in Latin and English with Notes*
RM	*The Rule of the Master*

ABBREVIATIONS OF BIBLICAL BOOKS REFERRED TO IN THIS WORK

Old Testament

1 Chr.	1 Chronicles	*Isa.*	Isaiah
Dan.	Daniel	*Prov.*	Proverbs
Deut.	Deuteronomy	*Ps.*	Psalm
Eze.	Ezekiel	*1 Sam.*	1 Samuel
Gen.	Genesis		

Apocrypha

Sir.	Sirach (also known as Ecclesiasticus)	*Tob.*	Tobit

New Testament

1 Cor.	1 Corinthians	*Eph.*	Ephesians
2 Cor.	2 Corinthians	*Gal.*	Galatians

Matt.	Matthew	*Rom.*	Romans
1 Pet.	1 Peter	*1 Thess.*	1 Thessalonians
Phil.	Philippians	*1 Tim.*	1 Timothy
Rev.	Revelation	*2 Tim.*	2 Timothy

Prologue

1. *father*: There is some controversy with regard to *RB* over the words 'master' and 'father' which may refer either to Christ and God, or to the abbot of the monastery. It is also possible that 'master' refers to the author of *RM*: see Introduction, p. xxi.

2. *prophet*: Benedict uses this word to apply to any of the Old Testament prophets such as Isaiah or Ezekiel, and to the author of the psalms.

3. *Apostle*: This is only used for St Paul.

4. *school*: In this paragraph Benedict uses the words *schola* (school) and *monasterium* (monastery), both of which he takes over from *RM*, whose author uses them at the end of his psalm commentary which concludes his Prologue. 'School' definitely has connotations here of instruction, discipline and progress, while 'monastery' was used in Latin from the fourth century to mean either a cell, i.e. the habitation of a single hermit, or a building in which several monks lived, and it was also applied to a community of monks (cf. Cassian, *Conferences*, 18.10).

1 The kinds of monks

1. *monks*: The Latin *monachus*, translated as 'monk', is itself a translation from a Greek word which became popular in the fourth century to refer to those living a life devoted to God whether in solitude or in community. Current opinion holds that the original meaning seems to have been 'single', in the sense of 'unmarried' rather than 'alone'. It was first used in the Latin translation of the immensely influential *Life of Antony* by Athanasius, made in the 370s; see e.g. the Preface (*ECL* p. 7). On monastic terminology generally, see *RB 1980*, pp. 301–21. Benedict uses the word generically of all those living some kind of monastic life, whether solitary or in community. (Cf. 'monastery' in Prologue, note 4.)

   Coenobita, referring to those who live in community, is derived from the Greek *koinos bios* meaning 'common life'. *Anachorita* is derived from a Greek word meaning 'one who withdraws', while *heremita* means 'one who lives in the desert'. *Sarabaita*, mentioned by Cassian (*Conferences*, 18.7), may originally have been a non-pejorative Coptic word for 'monastic people'. *Gyrovagi* – meaning those who wander around, referring to itinerant monks – is only found in *RM* and *RB*; they are the subject of a long satire in *RM*, 1.

As to the kinds of monks, *RM* also lists four and uses the same words as *RB*. Jerome, in Letter 22 (*The Letters of St Jerome*, trans. C. C. Mierow, Ancient Christian Writers, 33 (London: Longman, Green and Co./Westminster, Maryland: Newman Press, 1963), pp. 169–73), written in about 384 to the young girl Eustochium, had distinguished three kinds of monks: anchorites, coenobites and 'remnuoth' who seem to be similar to Benedict's sarabaites. Cassian (*Conferences*, 18.4–8) first talks of three kinds of monks (anchorites, coenobites and sarabaites) and then adds a fourth, more recent, kind who think they do not need to obey anyone and who seek out remote cells so they can live as they like, in an undisciplined and sloppy manner.

2 *What kind of man the abbot should be*

1. *Abba*: Aramaic for 'father'. Christ uses 'Abba' at Mark 14:36, and it is picked up by St Paul at Rom. 8:15 and Gal. 4:6.
2. *Eli*: For the story of Eli and his failure to stop his sons' wicked behaviour, see 1 Sam. 2:12–4:18.

6 *Restraint of speech*

1. *superior*: The Latin word used here is *prior* which seems to refer to anyone who is older or higher in rank than the person making the request. The same word is used in this sense in Chapters 6, 7, 13, 20, 38, 40, 43, 53, 63, 68 and 71. In Chapter 7 the word *major* is also used, apparently in the same sense. The Latin word that came to be the technical term for the English 'prior' is *praepositus*, used in Chapters 21, 62, 65 and 71. *RM* uses *praepositus* much more frequently than *RB*, but restricts the use of *prior* (in Chapter 93) to refer to the abbot's predecessor. On the question of rank within the monastery, see Chapter 63.

7 Humility

1. *the ladder ... and ascending*: Jacob's dream is found in Gen. 28:12, and is also referred to in *RM* 10 but not in Cassian, *Conferences*.

2. *'A man's thought will confess to you'*: This is a translation of the Latin translation of the Greek (Septuagint) version of Ps. 75:11. The corresponding English verse (Ps. 76:10) is from the differently worded Hebrew version.

3. *'Self-indulgence ... the prize'*: It would seem that this is not biblical, but derives from the account of the martyrdom of the three sisters Agape, Chionia and Irene, put to death on 1 April 304 (*Bibliotheca Hagiographica Latina*, no. 118 in the collection of saints' lives known as the *Acta Sanctorum* (Paris, 1863–), originally conceived by Heribert Rosweyde in the early seventeenth century (see Chapter 42, note 1)).

4. *'The wise man ... few words'*: In *The Sentences of Sextus*, ed. H. Chadwick (Cambridge: Cambridge University Press, 1959), p. 29. This work was included among the ascetic texts found at Nag Hammadi in Egypt. They were translated into Latin by Rufinus (a prolific and influential translator of theological texts from Greek into Latin) around 400. *RM* quotes two of the sayings attributed to the shadowy figure of Sextus (*RM* 9 and 10, and *RM* 11), while Benedict only includes the first.

5. *the work of God*: The expression usually used throughout the *RB* for the communal prayer of the monastery, consisting of psalms, readings, hymns and prayers. See also Introduction, note 4.

8 The divine office at night

1. *the eighth hour of the night*: For the Romans, the hours of the day differed in length, depending on the time of year. Within each 24-hour period, light and darkness were always divided into twelve, but in summer, when there was more daylight, each hour of the daytime was longer and each hour of the night shorter, and vice versa in winter. The eighth hour of night, for example, would be eight hours after nightfall.

2. *night office*: The Latin *Vigiliae* (here 'night office') is sometimes translated as 'Matins'. The Latin *Matutinae* is translated in this volume as Lauds. See also Introduction, note 3.

9 The number of psalms to be said at the night office

1. *verse*: In the liturgical context of *RB*, Chapters 9–18, the Latin *versus* is translated 'verse'. Some translations give 'versicle'. In this context 'verse' refers to some verse of Scripture, usually from the Psalms, and often divided between statement and response. A verse can be inserted at various points in the liturgy. Benedict does not usually specify the verse to be used, except in the case of Ps. 51:15 in Chapter 9, and Ps. 70:1 in Chapter 17. In Chapter 43 'verse' seems also to be used to refer to the blessing and grace said before and after the meal.

2. *Gloria*: Refers to the first word of the Latin version of the so-called Lesser Doxology, which in English is 'Glory be to the Father and to the Son and to the Holy Spirit, as it was in the beginning, is now and ever shall be, world without end.' This provided an opportunity to express commitment to the Trinity.

3. *antiphon*: There is some confusion as to the meaning of this word. It might indicate a short chant sung after each psalm or interpolated between each verse or group of verses within the psalm. The words of the antiphon were probably taken from the psalm itself or from another passage of Scripture. Benedict gives no specific examples.

4. *Ambrosian hymns*: Hymns either written by St Ambrose, bishop of Milan at the end of the fourth century, or written in the same verse form of four octosyllabic lines, this being the most common hymn form in the Middle Ages.

5. *responsories*: A responsory, like the verse and antiphon, was a short passage of Scripture, possibly involving statement and response. It is the term applied specifically to the verse said after each reading.

6. *catholic*: This word means more or less the same as 'orthodox', implying that the recommended writers belong to the main body of the Christian church and not to a minority sect or heresy.

7. *Alleluia*: 'Praise God' (Hebrew).

8. *Kyrie Eleison*: 'Lord, have mercy' (Greek), followed by 'Christ, have mercy, Lord, have mercy.' The use of this phrase in the liturgy does not seem to have been common before Benedict's time.

10 *Arrangements for the night office in summer*

1. *1 November*: Whereas in *RM* the year is broadly divided in two between Easter and 24 September (as the autumn equinox), Benedict variously divides it between Easter and 13 September (Chapter 41, with reference to meal times) or 1 October (Chapter 48, with reference to times of manual labour and silent reading) or 1 November (here, with reference to readings in the divine office).

11 *The night office on Sundays*

1. *three canticles from the prophets*: Isaiah 12, Hezekiah (Isa. 38:10–20) and Habakkuk 3:2–19. A canticle is a song or prayer derived from the Bible; see also Chapter 12, note 3.
2. *Te Deum laudamus*: The two hymns were added by Benedict to the liturgy of the night office on Sundays to frame the Gospel reading: *Te Deum laudamus* ('We praise you, O God') is western, while *Te decet laus* ('It is right to praise you') derives from the eastern Christian tradition.

12 *The office of Lauds*

1. *Benedicite*: The so-called Song of the Three Holy Children, part of the story of the three Hebrew exiles put in the fiery furnace by Nebuchadnezzar, is included in the Apocrypha as a continuation of Daniel (3:57–88), and opens with the word 'Benedicite' in the Latin version. (See 'Biblical references and translation' in Note on the Text.)
2. *Psalms 148 to 150*: Suitable for Lauds ('Praises'), to which they give their name, because they all have the word 'praise' in their opening verse (as do Psalms 145–7). On the other services, see Introduction, p. viii and note 3 and Chapter 15, note 1.
3. *a canticle from the Gospel*: Refers to the prophecy of Zacharias, father of John the Baptist, about his son, in Luke 1:68–79. Other Gospel canticles were the *Magnificat* (Luke 1:46–55) and the *Nunc Dimittis* (Luke 2:29–32).

13 *Arrangements for Lauds on ordinary days*

1. *canticle from Deuteronomy*: Refers to the Song of Moses found in Deut. 32:1–43.
2. *final part*: I.e. 'Lead us not into temptation.'

15 *The times for saying the Alleluia*

1. *None*: In the daily routine of many monastic orders, None came to be celebrated directly after the main Mass of the day: from this practice comes the English use of the word 'noon' (deriving from None, originally the ninth hour, i.e. around mid-afternoon) to mean 'midday'.

17 *The number of psalms to be said at these hours*

1. *'God, come to my assistance'*: According to Cassian (*Conferences*, 10.10) repetition of this phrase was the best way to practise unceasing prayer.

18 *The order of the psalms*

1. *Psalms 4, 91 and 133*: Each of these brings out a different aspect of night, so they are particularly suitable for recitation during the evening office of Compline.
2. *whole week*: *Lives of the Fathers* (Book 5.4.57) includes a story illustrating the simple dedication of the early desert fathers to the recitation of all the psalms: 'A hermit came to see another hermit, who cooked a few lentils and said: "Let us worship God and then eat." One of them recited the whole psalter. The other read and meditated upon two of the greater prophets. In the morning the visitor went away and they had forgotten to eat the food' (*The Desert Fathers*, trans. Benedicta Ward, p. 29).

23 *Excommunication for offences*

1. *excommunicated*: Usually thought to involve exclusion from the sacraments, but Benedict also uses it to refer to the lesser punishment of exclusion from the shared meal.

27 *The abbot's care for the excommunicated*

1. *'senpectae'*: A strange word, which Benedict clearly interprets as referring to a mature and sympathetic person, it has been explained in various ways: as related to a word for a mustard-poultice, (used for healing), or from the Greek *sympaiktes*, meaning a companion.

38 *The weekly reader*

1. *Holy Communion*: *Mixtum* has been taken to mean a drink of diluted wine, or a light meal of bread and water or wine. In *RM*, 24 it is *merum*, i.e. undiluted wine, with the explanation that this is given to the reader after taking Communion but before he reads the lesson, to wash away any of the sacrament from his mouth so that he would not accidentally spit any of it out while reading. In Lanfranc's *Monastic Constitutions* (p. 8), written some five centuries after *RB*, *mixtum* is explicitly said to be a light meal consisting of food and drink.

40 *The proper amount of drink*

1. *drink*: In the *Lives of the Fathers* (Book 5.4.31), some brothers told Abba Poemen (or Pastor) of another brother who did not drink wine, to which his response was 'Wine is not for monks' (*The Desert Fathers*, trans. Ward, p. 25). In the Life of Martin of Tours by Sulpicius Severus we see that he only allowed his monks to drink a little wine for medicinal purposes (10, *ECL* p. 144). However, it seems to have become the norm for monks to have wine: we see, for example, how unpopular the eighth-century monk Guthlac became with his brothers when he refused to drink any wine (Felix, *Life of St Guthlac*, ed. B. Colgrave, Cambridge: Cambridge University Press, 1956, p. 84).

41 *Meal times*

1. *13 September*: See Chapter 10, note 1.

42 *Silence after Compline*

1. *the Conferences or the Lives of the Fathers*: The *Conferences* are by John Cassian, while the title *Lives of the Fathers* (known in Latin as *Vitae Patrum*) refers to a collection of stories about and sayings of the desert fathers, most of which were originally collected in Greek but probably translated into Latin at Rome very shortly before Benedict advocated their use in his monasteries. There are different versions of this collection which was popular throughout the Middle Ages, often attributed to Jerome, but it only acquired the form it now has in the *PL* (vols. 73 and 74) through the edition of the Jesuit Heribert Rosweyde in the

early seventeenth century. We do not know exactly what was in the collection Benedict knew. It may only have been the collection of sayings (known in Latin as *Verba Seniorum* or *Admonitiones*) of the desert fathers now contained in Book 5 of the *Lives of the Fathers* (*PL* 73, columns 855–1022), for he definitely seems to be alluding to two stories contained in that book (see Chapters 18, note 2 and 40, note 1). Book 5 may only have been translated into Latin by the deacon Pelagius (who became Pope Pelagius I in 556) in the 540s, in which case Benedict would have come to know of it very late in life, quickly recognizing its potential as an inspirational text for the monks. (Book 5 has been translated into English by Benedicta Ward as *The Desert Fathers*.)

In *RM*, probably written in the first quarter of the sixth century, the *Lives of the Fathers* is mentioned in Chapter 26: the author says the abbot can even provide sweets for the monks on feast-days or if guests are present, 'in accordance with the Lives of the Fathers, where one reads that on feast days they asked the Lord for tasty food and then an angel with a honey-comb appeared to them'. This seems to be an allusion to Chapter 7 of the *History of the Monks in Egypt*, an account of a visit to Egypt made in about 395 by Timotheus of Alexandria and translated into Latin by Rufinus around 400 (*The Lives of the Desert Fathers*, trans. Norman Russell). It is clear that the title *Lives of the Fathers* could be used to apply to various works and collections dating from the fourth century and later.

2. *Heptateuch . . . Kings*: The Heptateuch is the first seven books of the Old Testament, while Kings refers to the four historical books of the Old Testament in its Latin version, which in the English texts are called 1 and 2 Samuel, 1 and 2 Kings.

46 Offences committed elsewhere

1. *loses it*: Not all monks who obeyed Benedict's order to report the breakage or loss of any tool were as fortunate as the young monk in his own monastery as told by Gregory in *Life of Benedict*, 6 (*ECL* pp. 174–5). This monk had been given a tool to clear away brambles from a proposed garden area, but when he 'attacked the thick brambles energetically, the metal tool shot out from the handle and fell into the lake'. With no hope of retrieving it the monk obediently reported the breakage and loss. Benedict took the broken handle, went down to the lake and plunged it in. The metal blade miraculously jumped out of the

water and fitted back into the handle, and Benedict handed the tool back to the young monk, telling him calmly not to be upset but to resume his work.

48 Daily manual labour

1. *biblical study*: The Latin phrase *lectio divina* has been translated in many ways: for example, 'godly', 'divine' or 'prayerful reading' or 'reading devoted to God'. In fact it would seem from other Latin texts of the early Christian period that it originally meant 'Bible reading', and Benedict may well have intended it to refer to the reading of the Bible and Bible commentaries. He seems to envisage individual study by the monks, in contrast to *RM*, 50, which recommends that each of the monastery's deans should read aloud for three hours to the ten monks for whom he is responsible, while the boys and any monks up to the age of fifty who are illiterate should spend the time learning to read and write. Individual Bible study was not restricted to those living in a monastery: St Augustine, for example, in Letter 20 (*The Confessions and Letters of St. Augustin*, trans. P. Schaff, in The Nicene and Post-Nicene Fathers of the Christian Church, first series (Edinburgh: T. and T. Clark/Grand Rapids, Michigan: Wm. B. Eerdmans, reprinted, 1994), vol. 1), written in about 390, advises Antoninus to use *lectio divina* and serious conversations to instil in his wife a rational fear of God.

57 The monastery craftsmen

1. *Ananias and Saphira*: They kept back part of the proceeds of property they sold, all of which were meant to be distributed to people in need (Acts 5:1–11).

63 Rank within the community

1. *Samuel and Daniel*: On Samuel and his criticism of Eli, see 1 Samuel 3. Daniel's rebuke of his elders occurs in the apocryphal book of Susanna (Dan. 13:44–62): it is one of the three stories found in the Greek text of Daniel, but not in the Hebrew.
2. *'nonnus'*: This is the Latin form of a rare Greek word for 'father' and seems to have been used as a term of respect. In its Latin form it had been used by Jerome (Letter 117, in St Jerome, *Letters and Selected Works*, trans. H. Wace and P. Schaff, in The Nicene

and Post-Nicene Fathers of the Christian Church, second series (Oxford: Parker, 1893; reprinted Edinburgh: T. and T. Clark/ Grand Rapids, Michigan: Wm. B. Eerdmans, 1994), vol. 6), to refer to a monk or holy man in the early fifth century. The feminine form of this word, 'nonna', gives us the English word 'nun'.

73 *This rule is only a start on the path to justice*

1. *Institutes . . . Basil*: The *Institutes*, like the *Conferences*, were the work of John Cassian: see Introduction, p. xx. St Basil wrote his monastic rules in the third quarter of the fourth century: see Introduction, p. xvii.

THE STORY OF PENGUIN CLASSICS

Before 1946 ... 'Classics' are mainly the domain of academics and students; readable editions for everyone else are almost unheard of. This all changes when a little-known classicist, E. V. Rieu, presents Penguin founder Allen Lane with the translation of Homer's *Odyssey* that he has been working on in his spare time.

1946 Penguin Classics debuts with *The Odyssey*, which promptly sells three million copies. Suddenly, classics are no longer for the privileged few.

1950s Rieu, now series editor, turns to professional writers for the best modern, readable translations, including Dorothy L. Sayers's *Inferno* and Robert Graves's unexpurgated *Twelve Caesars*.

1960s The Classics are given the distinctive black covers that have remained a constant throughout the life of the series. Rieu retires in 1964, hailing the Penguin Classics list as 'the greatest educative force of the twentieth century.'

1970s A new generation of translators swells the Penguin Classics ranks, introducing readers of English to classics of world literature from more than twenty languages. The list grows to encompass more history, philosophy, science, religion and politics.

1980s The Penguin American Library launches with titles such as *Uncle Tom's Cabin*, and joins forces with Penguin Classics to provide the most comprehensive library of world literature available from any paperback publisher.

1990s The launch of Penguin Audiobooks brings the classics to a listening audience for the first time, and in 1999 the worldwide launch of the Penguin Classics website extends their reach to the global online community.

The 21st Century Penguin Classics are completely redesigned for the first time in nearly twenty years. This world-famous series now consists of more than 1300 titles, making the widest range of the best books ever written available to millions – and constantly redefining what makes a 'classic'.

The Odyssey continues ...

The best books ever written

PENGUIN CLASSICS

SINCE 1946

Find out more at www.penguinclassics.com